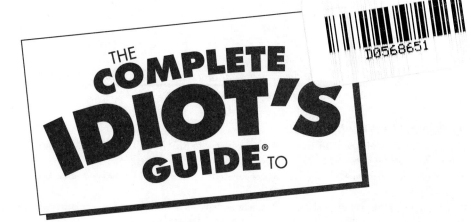

THE COMPLETE IDIOT'S GUIDE® TO

Home Recording

Illustrated

by Clayton Walnum

ALPHA

A member of Penguin Group (USA) Inc.

To all the amazing people whose technical contributions have made today's home recording studios possible.

Publisher: *Marie Butler-Knight*
Product Manager: *Phil Kitchel*
Senior Managing Editor: *Jennifer Chisholm*
Senior Acquisitions Editor: *Mike Sanders*
Development Editor: *Tom Stevens*
Senior Production Editor: *Christy Wagner*
Copy Editor: *Keith Cline*
Illustrator: *Chris Eliopoulos*
Cover/Book Designer: *Trina Wurst*
Indexer: *Brad Herriman*
Layout: *Becky Harmon*

Contents at a Glance

Contents

Foreword

The art of recording certainly has changed! Since I started Trod Nossel Recording Studios back in 1968, the state of the art has gone from 4-track recorders to mind-boggling digital machines that can accommodate 128 tracks and more. As the pro studios improved, so did the recording equipment available to the home-based musician. Presently, you can purchase a recording workstation—"studio-in-a-box"—that has almost as much power as my entire studio had a couple decades ago.

Recording, however, is both an art and a science. As with all art, you must practice to perfect your skills. And as with all sciences, you need to learn the rules that govern the recording universe—I mean the rules that make the difference between a masterful recording and a mediocre one. That's what this book is all about—learning to use the tools available to the amateur recording engineer/enthusiast. And although these home recording tools can never produce the type of recording you can get in a pro studio, they can take you a long way toward that goal. In fact, it's not unusual for musicians to bring their home-recording projects into Trod Nossel Recording Studios, where they can be professionally mixed and mastered.

Clayton Walnum, this book's author, has been recording music for more than 30 years. I know this because he received some of his first training right here at Trod Nossel Studios. At that time, he was a young guitarist whose band played in New England–area clubs. More important, he was (and is) a musician with an unquenchable desire to learn everything he could about recording. After his classes here at the studio, he returned often to record, engineer, and produce his own songs. He also set up and engineered sessions for other bands in the area. Over the years, he's moved from one band to another, but has always continued his studies of the recording arts.

Now, you, the reader, can take advantage of all Clay has learned over the years. Thanks to the proliferation of computer-based recording software such as Pro Tools, you can set up your own start-up studio and follow along as Clay tells you everything you need to know to record and mix your own songs, right at home. No need to worry about wordy and hi-tech discourses on mind-boggling topics that only a professional audio engineer can understand. Clay delivers just the information you need and does so in a disarming and often humorous tone. You'll never have so much fun reading a technical book.

Thomas "Doc" Cavalier

Thomas "Doc" Cavalier is owner and CEO of Trod Nossel Artists, a complex of music-related entities based in Wallingford, Connecticut, that includes Trod Nossel Recording Studios. Founded in 1968, the studio is one of the longest-running recording facilities in the world. Clients who have enjoyed production services at Trod Nossel include Fleetwood Mac, Donovan, the Rolling Stones, the Wildweeds, Steppenwolf, Taj Majal, B. Willie Smith, The Scratch Band, Chick Corea, Eddie Kirkland, Pinetop Perkins, Roger McGuinn, former Brownsville Station member Cub Koda, Christine Ohlman, and Rebel Montez, as well as Motown's Rare Earth label. Many of Cavalier's productions were accorded worldwide release via a link with the British Decca/London labels.

www.doccavalier.com
www.trodnossel.com

Introduction

It wasn't that long ago that if you wanted to record a song, you had to go to a professional studio and pay between $50 and $300 an hour for their services. Obviously, the time and expense involved prohibited most people from ever experiencing the thrill of recording a song of their own. Thanks to the digital revolution, though—not to mention the continually downward-spiraling cost of electronic equipment—you can set up a complete studio in your own home for less than it would have cost you to rent that pro studio for a few hours. Amazingly, you can get started for next to nothing!

Of course, having a studio and using it are two different things. To record and mix your songs, you need to develop a whole list of skills, including using multitrack recorders, selecting the right microphones, setting up equipment properly, processing sound with equalizers and compressors, editing recorded performances, and so much more.

Luckily, if you're willing to spend a little time reading and experimenting, you can learn quickly at least the basic skills needed to produce professional-sounding recordings. Whether you just want to record that song that's been kicking around in your head or whether you want to produce a full CD for your band, the same skills apply. In this book, you'll find everything you need to know.

Who This Book Is For

Although the information contained in these pages is mostly useful to musicians who want to produce their own music, anyone can benefit from—not to mention have a lot of fun with—the techniques taught here. If you're just curious about the process of recording and mixing modern songs, you can discover all the basic secrets for the price of this book. If you also have a computer, you can even try it all out for yourself.

Here's a list of people who will get the most from this book:

◆ Amateur musicians who want to record songs as a hobby

◆ Professional musicians who want to produce demo recordings or CDs for sale

◆ Music lovers who want to try their hand at writing and recording their own music

◆ Anyone who's interested in what's involved in producing music in a studio

As you can tell from this list, about the only requirement for enjoying this book is enjoying music itself!

How This Book Is Organized

The information in this book is broken down into several main topics, as follows:

Part 1, "Getting Started with Recording," gives you an overview of the entire music production process, covers the equipment you might want, and shows you how to set up your computer for recording and mixing music.

Part 2, "The Recording Process," shows you how to record your music as a multitrack project, with each instrument isolated on its own track for maximum flexibility. You also discover how to use effects during recording, and how to turn problem performances into finished tracks.

Part 3, "The Mixing Process," teaches you how to take your multitrack project and convert it to a stereo sound file that can be played on conventional music equipment, such as your home stereo system or portable CD player.

Extras

You'll also find the following boxed tips and information throughout the book:

Notes from the Track Sheet

These boxes present additional information about the topic at hand. This information will either add to your understanding or provide interesting side discussions.

Just Push Play

These boxes offer valuable tips that make recording projects easier and more fun, and may even get you out of a jam or two.

Acknowledgments

The author would like to thank all the fine folks who helped make this book a reality. Those folks include, but are not limited to, Marie Butler-Knight, Eric Heagy, Mike Sanders, Tom Stevens, Christy Wagner, and Keith Cline. A big thank you to Dan "Dano" Palladino for checking the technical accuracy of this book's contents and for providing helpful suggestions. A similarly big thank you to Christopher Walnum for reading each chapter for clarity. As always, thanks to the whole Walnum clan, including Lynn, Chris, Justin, Stephen, and Caitlynn.

Special Thanks to the Technical Reviewer

The Complete Idiot's Guide to Home Recording Illustrated was reviewed by an expert who double-checked the accuracy of what you'll learn here, to help us ensure that this book gives you everything you need to know about home recording. Special thanks are extended to Dan Palladino.

Trademarks

All terms mentioned in this book that are known to be or are suspected of being trademarks or service marks have been appropriately capitalized. Alpha Books and Penguin Group (USA) Inc. cannot attest to the accuracy of this information. Use of a term in this book should not be regarded as affecting the validity of any trademark or service mark.

In This Part

Part 1

Getting Started with Recording

Before you dip your foot into the waters of home recording, you might want to warm the pool up a bit. In this part of the book, we do that by learning the general methods by which recordings are produced. This means learning about the types of equipment you may run into, as well as what the whole concept of multitrack recording means to you.

Because this book demonstrates recording principles using a computer-based studio setup, this introductory part also digs into the type of computer you need, including the speed of the processor and the quality of the sound card. Chances are, you already have what you need. If not, you learn where and how to get the equipment you need. You even discover how to get free recording software.

Finally, in this part, you learn to connect your computer to other types of hardware, not the least of which is a monitoring system that you can use to listen to your recordings. From headphones to home stereos to full-fledged studio monitoring systems, it's all covered here. We even tackle microphones, without which you won't get far.

In This Chapter

- ◆ Exploring all-in-one workstations and recording components

- ◆ Choosing a computer-based recording system

- ◆ Exploring all-in-one music workstations

- ◆ A quick look at some popular music software

Chapter 1

Introduction to Home Recording

Whether you're a professional musician, a skilled amateur, or just someone interested in dabbling with songwriting and recording, there's a home recording system perfect for you. You can get started with this fascinating and rewarding hobby for next to nothing or spend thousands of dollars. The choice is yours. However, the number of choices is truly mind-boggling. The home recording market offers thousands of products to people just like you. No lie! Never in the history of music have there been so many ways to create and record your own songs.

In this chapter, you start on this wonderful journey by looking at some of the leading products designed specifically for the home recording enthusiast. Here, you get a glance at everything from tiny pocket recorders to full-fledged studio-in-a-box systems. Of course, because most of this book concentrates on computer-based studios, you also get a quick look at some of the top recording software.

Which Way to Go?

When it comes to choosing a system for home recording, you can take several routes. Your main choices are as follows:

◆ All-in-one workstations
◆ Individual components
◆ Computer-based workstation

The all-in-one workstations are mini-home studios that provide everything you need to record your own masterpieces. Usually such systems include not only a recorder, but also effects, CD burners, and more. If you have a hard time picturing such a machine, think of home stereo equipment. You know those stereo systems that include a cassette player, a CD player, a radio, an amplifier, and speakers all built in to one box? The all-in-one music workstations are the home recording version of such systems, except they don't usually come with speakers. Figure 1.1 shows an all-in-one workstation.

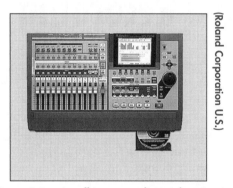

Figure 1.2 shows a set of hardware components for a home studio setup. The figure shows a reverberation unit, a compressor, and an equalizer. If you don't know what some of this stuff is, you will by the end of this book. I promise!

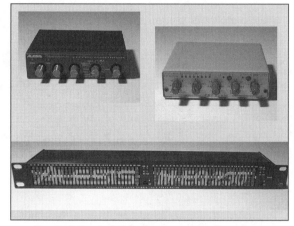

Figure 1.2   Individual components for a home studio.

(Roland Corporation U.S.)

Figure 1.1   An all-in-one audio workstation.

Continuing with the home stereo comparison, if you want more flexibility, you can buy a cassette player, a CD player, a radio, an amplifier, and speakers as separate components. The same is true with home studio equipment. You can buy each component separately—including a recorder, a mixer, effects, and monitors—and assemble exactly the system you want. Usually such a system is more expensive than the all-in-one choice and requires some expertise in order to purchase compatible components and connect them properly.

In between these two extremes is the computer-based system. In this case, you purchase audio software that turns your computer into the equivalent of an all-in-one box. Assembling such a system does require a little knowledge, but the results can be much more flexible and powerful than the standalone all-in-one workstations. If you already have a computer, the computer-based system is also the most inexpensive way to get started with home recording. For all of these reasons, the majority of this book deals with the computer-based home studio.

In the rest of this chapter, you'll examine some of the recording systems available for the home studio, including all-in-one systems and computer-based systems. This book features very little coverage of the component-based systems, because such systems are better left to those with more experience.

Notes from the Track Sheet

Currently, the all-in-one type of audio workstation is the most popular with hobbyist recording folks, because such a system is compact, all its components are guaranteed compatible, and setting it up is just a matter of plugging in the power cord and connecting a set of speakers.

However, the all-in-one boxes can be exceedingly confusing to use. To lower their costs and to keep the design compact, most of the controls have multiple uses depending on the current mode of operation. Many functions don't even have physical controls and must be set on a tiny LCD screen. This is a lot like having a computer with a three-inch monitor. And trying to remember where a setting is located in the complex, nested menus is enough to drive you mad.

More and more people, amateurs and professionals alike, are moving to computer-based systems, due to the lower expense (assuming the person already owns a suitable computer) and the added flexibility. And that's not to mention a full-size, color monitor in place of a three-inch, monochrome LCD!

Home Recording the Old-Fashioned Way

Not all that long ago (maybe 15 years or so), the only inexpensive option for someone who wanted to record music at home was the cassette-based mini-recorder. Perhaps the most famous of these machines was the Tascam Portastudio, a clever machine that used ordinary cassette tapes to record and mix music. Portastudios (and their imitators) were four-track machines, which means that you could record four different instruments on one tape and then mix them together to create a final song.

You can still get a cassette-based Portastudio, and such a machine is probably your cheapest way to get started with recording (unless you already own a computer). You can grab one of these brand new for a street price of around $100. But as the saying goes, you get what you pay for. Such an inexpensive machine doesn't have a lot of options, and you may quickly outgrow it. Other cassette-based machines go for between $200 and $300 at most music stores.

Trust me, though, when I say that cassette-based machines are only appropriate for folks who want to experiment with music recording, but don't care about the sound quality of the result. Although it's possible to get a decent recording out of a cassette-based machine, it's an uphill battle—in fact, it's more like an uphill battle with an elephant strapped to your back. On top of the poor recording quality, you have to deal with a lot of tape hiss, which is one of the downsides of using analog recording tape of any type, but especially with cassettes, although Dolby noise reduction systems help keep the hiss almost tolerable.

Moving Into the Digital Age

Once digital recorders entered the marketplace at a price that most people could afford, the cassette-based machines became as antiquated as great-grandma's rocking chair. Today, four-track digital machines cost about the same as the cassette-based machines used to cost. One example is the Boss BR-532 Digital Studio, shown in Figure 1.3, which you can pick up for a street price of about $350. This type of four-track machine uses a hard disk to store music, rather than any kind of tape. You also get a lot more bang for the buck than you used to get with the cassette-based type of recorder.

(Roland Corporation U.S.)

Figure 1.3   Boss BR-532 Digital Studio.

When you're only looking for three or four tracks, you can get along with one of the new so-called pocket studios. I use a Zoom PS-02 (Figure 1.4) for a lot of my songwriting. This way-cool machine is about the size of a pack of cards (but a bit thicker), records onto tiny memory cards, and runs on batteries. It offers three-track recording, as well as a built-in drum machine, bass-guitar lines, and a complete set of guitar effects, such as distortion and echo: an amazing piece of hardware for around $300.

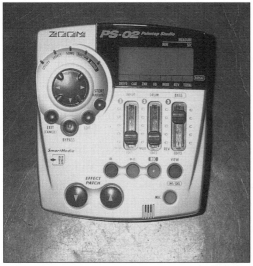

Figure 1.4   The Zoom PS-02 three-track digital recorder.

Tascam has a similar machine that they tout as the Portastudio for the new millennium. Called Pocketstudio 5, this baby is a four-track machine, also with tons of effects, but with a price tag between $400 and $500. One cool thing is how the Pocketstudio 5 can send your finished song to your computer as an MP3 file. You can even use the machine as a portable MP3 player.

Once you're ready to get serious about recording, you're going to want to have at least eight tracks to work with, and you're going to need a lot more power than you can get with the smaller recorders. Still, you can get eight-track all-in-one boxes for very reasonable prices these days, though nowhere near as cheap as the four-track machines.

Tascam offers the 788 Digital Portastudio (Figure 1.5) for those who want more power and tracks than those offered by the smaller machines and who have the $800 or so it takes to purchase one of these marvels. As you can see from the picture, this range of machine can get pretty complex and so can take a while to learn to use. Once you get the hang of it, though, you can turn out nearly studio-quality recordings, assuming you have the know-how (which is, of course, why you're reading this book!).

Figure 1.5   The Tascam 788 Digital Portastudio.

For about the same price, you can get the Boss BR-1180 10-Track Digital Recording Studio (Figure 1.6), the Korg D1200 Digital Recorder, or the Roland CDX-1 DiscLab Music Production Station, just to name a few.

(Roland Corporation U.S.)

Figure 1.6   Boss BR-1180 10-Track Digital Recording Studio.

Finally, if you're really serious about music recording, there are plenty of full-featured, nearly pro recording systems, but you'll have to lay out a pretty penny (or three) to buy them. Before moving to a computer-based studio, I used a Roland VS-1680, a 16-track machine that's been replaced by a 24-track version named VS-2480 (Figure 1.7), a marvel of modern technology that'll set you back more than $3,000.

(Roland Corporation U.S.)

Figure 1.7   The Roland VS-2480 24-track digital workstation.

Notes from the Track Sheet

As I mentioned, I used to do a lot of recording on the Roland VS-1680, 16-track machine. At the time, I was moving from a digital-tape system (an Alesis ADAT, for those who are curious) and loved the idea of no longer having to deal with any kind of tape. It didn't take long, though, before a computer-based system was the obvious way to go. Such a system has everything the VS-1680 has and a whole lot more. Although my VS-1680 was a great machine, my new computer system with Pro Tools blows it away!

Other similar machines include the Yamaha AW2816 Audio Workstation, which goes for about $2,000, all the way up to the Tascam SX-1 Digital Audio Production Station, whose $9,000 price tag will empty your wallet for a long time to come. And of course, there are machines that cost even more.

Moving On to the Computer

Yep, you can spend a ton of money on recording equipment. However, if you own a reasonably powerful computer, you may already have made the biggest investment you need to get started with home recording. Many companies offer sophisticated software that turns your computer into a full-fledged recording workstation, one that can be even more powerful than the machines at which you just looked.

Such software ranges in price from less than $100 to more than $700. One example is the popular *Cakewalk Sonar*, which goes for about $500, but you can get a "lite" version called *Cakewalk Home Studio* for a mere $100. Another popular choice is Steinberg's *Cubase*, which has a street price of around $800.

But the granddaddy of them all is Digidesign's *Pro Tools* (Figure 1.8), software that's considered standard fare in major recording studios. Pro Tools comes in various versions, with price tags as high as $13,000 for a complete system. But here's the good news: Digidesign offers a version of Pro Tools that's completely free! Because of this more-than-reasonable price tag, we'll be using Pro Tools

Free throughout this book to demonstrate the many recording techniques you need to learn.

And this concludes your quick tour of the home recording products from which an aspiring songwriter can choose. As you can see, you have many ways to go, but the best way to get started—not to mention the best way to put together one of the most flexible home recording systems on the planet—is to use your home computer as the starting point. For the rest of this book, the computer-based home recording studio is the focus of our attention. However, keep in mind that most of the recording techniques you'll learn are applicable to any recording setup. How can you beat that?

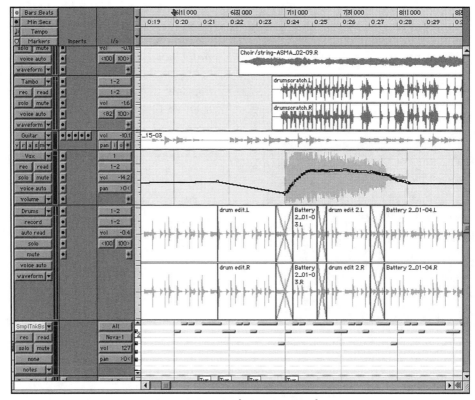

Figure 1.8   Digidesign's **Pro Tools.**

The Least You Need to Know

◆ When it comes to choosing a system for home recording, you can take several routes: all-in-one workstations, individual components, or a computer-based workstation.

◆ The all-in-one workstations are mini-home studios that provide everything you need to record your own masterpieces, but tend to be hard to use.

◆ When going the separate component route, you can assemble exactly the system you want. However, such a system is usually expensive and requires expertise in order to purchase compatible components and connect them properly.

◆ In the case of a computer-based system, you purchase audio software that turns your computer into the equivalent of an all-in-one box. If you already have a computer, this is the most inexpensive way to get started with home recording.

In This Chapter

◆ Understanding why a computer is a great investment for a home-studio enthusiast

◆ Exploring the minimum system requirements for a usable home-studio computer

◆ Ways to upgrade a computer system for a more powerful audio workstation

◆ Where to buy a computer and music software and hardware

Chapter 2

The Computer

In the previous chapter, you got a quick overview of some of the equipment available to you as a home recording hobbyist. You saw that you can invest very little in a system or as much as the national debt. (Okay, maybe not quite that much.) Most important, though, you discovered that if you already own a personal computer, you may be well on your way toward setting up your home recording studio for next to nothing, and that's a price tag I know we all can live with!

Even if you don't have a personal computer, a computer-based studio may be the best way to go, because the total investment won't be much more than buying a dedicated music workstation, and a computer can do a lot more than just record music. It can also run all the latest computer software, including word processors, games, web browsers, and so much more that a dedicated recording machine can't do. Dollar for dollar, a computer-based recording system is almost certainly your best bet.

In this chapter, then, you examine exactly the type of computer system that's appropriate for a home recording studio. Along the way, you discover how to upgrade your current system in preparation for setting up recording software; those without computers will find great advice on how to go about making this important investment.

What Does the Computer Need?

What extras your computer needs to record music depends on how far you want to go with your home recording studio. Believe it or not, you may be able to get started with recording just by installing the free version of Pro Tools and plugging a cheap microphone into your computer's sound card. This is enough of a computer studio to get you through most of the lessons in this book. So at the very minimum, you need the following:

- A PC with a 500MHz Pentium III or better processor (software may also run on equivalent AMD processors)
- Windows 98 Second Edition or Windows Me (Pro Tools Free currently does not run under Windows XP)
- Minimum of 128MB system RAM, 192MB recommended
- AGP or PCI graphics card
- Stereo sound card with a microphone input
- A monitor capable of a screen resolution of 1024×768
- A fast hard drive with plenty of free space

> **Notes from the Track Sheet**
>
> Pro Tools Free also comes in a version for Mac users, so don't feel left out if your system is a Mac. Although I use a PC system for the lessons in this book, almost everything discussed works identically on a Macintosh-based system.

Most computers purchased in the past few years should easily match these requirements, although you may have to boost your system RAM a bit.

How Many MHz Are Enough?

The abbreviation *MHz* stands for *megahertz*. A lot of you might be scratching your heads now. Some of you may have head lice, but the rest probably just don't know what MHz means even when it's spelled out, and that's okay. To avoid explaining a lot of scientific junk, I'll just say that the higher the hertz number for your computer, the faster the computer can do its work. For example, a 900MHz computer is faster than a 640MHz computer.

So how fast of a processor do you really need? That depends to some degree on the software you want to run and how hard you plan to drive your system, but a good rule of thumb is to get the best system you can afford. This is because you want to be able to run not only today's software, but also the software that may come out in the next year or two. The best new-computer bet at the moment would be a Pentium 4 computer running at around 2GHz (that's *gigahertz*, not megahertz). You can probably get such a computer for as little $1,000.

> **Notes from the Track Sheet**
>
> The term *mega* (M) means one million in that funky metric system they've been trying to stuff down our throats for the last few decades. On the other hand, *giga* (G) means one billion. *Hertz* is the measurement of how often a frequency completes a cycle. One hertz is a signal that completes a cycle once a second. Who cares, right?

If you're not concerned with the future (bad mistake, in my opinion, but hey, it's your life), you can get by with a lot less. A used computer running at around 750MHz ought to serve you well for most simple recording situations and not cost too much. I don't think you'll find a new one running at those speeds, though. That's pretty old technology.

System RAM

Closely related to the speed of the computer is the amount of memory available to your programs. A computer with 256MB of RAM can handle recording tasks a lot better than one with only 128MB. It's not unusual to see a new computer with 512MB of memory. The more the merrier! If you want your studio computer to handle your music needs for the next couple of years, 256MB should be the minimum amount of memory to go for and 512MB is recommended.

Just Push Play

These days, RAM is fairly cheap. Compared to 10 years ago, in fact, computer stores are practically giving it away. For that reason, adding RAM is often the most cost-effective way to boost your computer system's performance. Cram as many memory chips as you can into that machine! Just make sure you get the right ones. (Consult a technician when in doubt.)

The Sound Card

You don't need a state-of-the-art sound card to get started with recording, but the better your card, the better your sound quality. Most sound cards these days support stereo sound (I don't think you can even buy a new monophonic card anymore, but I could be wrong). Better cards support surround sound, just like a home theater system. Of course, in this book we're not even going to go *near* the subject of recording for surround sound. You've got enough to learn as it is. I only mention surround sound because it's cool for games. (Yeah, I'm an RPG geek.)

Although you can start with just about any sound card, many manufacturers make sound hardware especially for the computer-based home studio. Such sound hardware not only provides top-notch audio, but also plenty of places to plug in microphones, electronic instruments, and all the other stuff you'll eventually want to record.

In my studio, I use the Digidesign Digi 001 system (Figure 2.1), which has a street price of about $750. This system comes with the Pro Tools LE software, which is the next step up from Pro Tools Free, the software you'll use in this book.

The Digi 001 system is actually the "baby" home system. People with a bigger budget would no doubt opt for the new Digi 002 system, shown in Figure 2.2. This system, however, costs more than $2,000—and that's in addition to the cost of a computer system.

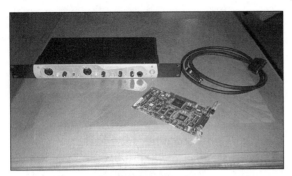

Figure 2.1   The Digidesign Digi 001 recording system for Pro Tools.

Figure 2.2   The Digidesign Digi 002 recording system for Pro Tools.

When it comes to sound cards, cheaper alternatives abound. Figure 2.3 shows Echo's Mia Digital Audio Card, which goes for a very reasonable $200. Echo also offers a system very similar to the Digi 001. Figure 2.4 shows front and back views of this system, which is named the Echo Layla 24/96 Multitrack Recording System. This hardware and software combo goes for about $750. (I owned the previous version of the Layla system and used it to interface between my Roland VS-1680 and my computer. Refer to the previous chapter if you've forgotten what a VS-1680 is.)

There are dozens of other choices, too. But you shouldn't get too caught up with hardware fever yet. (Heaven knows, I've got it bad enough for all of us! When I browse the catalogs, I have to keep a paper towel in hand to wipe the drool off the pages.) First, you need to understand the basics of recording and how to use the simpler stuff before you run out and spend a pile of dough on equipment that's as confusing as the controls on the space shuttle.

(Echo Digital Audio Corporation)

Figure 2.3 The Echo Mia Digital Audio Card.

(Echo Digital Audio Corporation)

Figure 2.4 The Echo Layla 24/96 Multitrack Recording System.

The Hard Disk

A very important part of the system is your computer's hard drive. The faster it is, the better it can keep up with the grueling data transfer that's typical of multitrack sound recording. And, the bigger the hard drive is, the more music it'll fit. Digital sound files run about 10MB per minute, and each track you record is a separate file. This means that a 3-minute, 8-track song eats up about 240MB of disk space.

Chances are that the hard drive currently in your system will suffice for now. (Or maybe not; you'll just have to see.) Most recording systems, however, strongly suggest a system with two hard drives, one drive for software, including your operating system and your studio software, and another drive for nothing except audio files. Having two drives makes the recording system much more efficient, not to mention gives you tons of room. You can get an 80GB drive these days for just a bit more than $100. And 80GB holds a lot of audio data! In fact, it'll hold as many as 320 of those 3-minute, 8-track songs we were talking about.

Where to Shop

Suppose you don't have a computer yet, or you want to upgrade your old one. Where should you buy your computer? You have several choices. Here's a list:

◆ A used-computer store
◆ A chain electronics store such as Radio Shack
◆ An electronics superstore such as CompUSA, Circuit City, or Best Buy
◆ A mail-order computer manufacturer such as Dell or Gateway

All of these types of computer stores have their advantages and disadvantages. However, my suggestion is that you go with the mail-order companies, for reasons we'll get into soon. But first, let's look at the other possibilities.

There are a lot of "mom and pop" used-computer stores out there, and you can get some really good deals if you know what you're looking for. However, there can be a huge downside to this type of computer shopping. First, most of the systems you'll find in such a store will be woefully outdated. That is, it may be tough to find a system that will meet the requirements for a good home-studio computer. Second, buying used computers is a lot like buying used cars. You never know exactly what you're getting, and you can't always rely on the salesperson to be honest. If you go this

route, at least be sure you get some sort of guarantee, although you're not likely to get anything beyond 30 days.

Your next choice is a small chain store, such as Radio Shack. In such a shop, you may or may not have salespeople who actually know what they're talking about, but chances are at least the store manager will be able to answer your questions. Again, having someone with you who knows the story is helpful. The prices at these types of shops are reasonable, and usually you can get a good guarantee and reasonable exchange policies.

Next on the list is the superstore, which includes not only computer superstores like CompUSA, but also general superstores like Circuit City and Best Buy. The prices in these places are pretty good, because they're constantly in competition with each other and usually have lowest-price guarantees. The biggest downside is that the systems in such stores come "prefab," meaning that you get whatever is in the box. You can't, for example, swap one sound card for another. Of course, the salesman will be perfectly happy to sell you a second sound card, as long as you're willing to eat the one already packaged with the system. (Mmmmmm! Crunchy!) They'll even be glad to charge you for the installation.

Just Push Play

Most places that sell computer systems do not sell pro audio software and components. To get that kind of stuff, you need to go to a major music store, such as Guitar Center or Sam Ash. You can also purchase your audio needs on the Internet, either directly from the companies that manufacture the equipment (an expensive way to go) or from major music stores, such as those just mentioned.

The other downside with the superstores is that, as is typical these days, it can be hard to find someone who knows what he's talking about. It's tough to get experts for the low wages these places pay, and low wages is just one of the ways they keep their prices down. What you gain on one end, you lose on the other.

You may think by what I've written in the previous paragraphs, that I have something against electronics superstores. Well, I do and I don't. You can do well in these places if you know what you're doing. Moreover, within an hour or so, you can walk out the door with your new system, rather than waiting for it to be custom assembled. The bottom line is that you can get a good computer system at a superstore. Just make a list of what you need in the system and stick to it.

My suggestion, though, is to go with a mail-order company such as Dell or Gateway. I favor Dell, myself, because I've had great luck with them and their customer service is beyond excellent. On Dell's website, you can custom build your computer part by part and see the total price as you add each component. Dell will then assemble the computer just as you requested and ship it to your front door.

With the mail-order companies, you can get great warranties that protect you for three years or more. Moreover, for a little extra payola, you can get home service, where they send a

technician right to your house within 24 hours to repair your system if something should go wrong. With simpler repairs, such as replacing a plug-in disk drive, they'll send you a new part by overnight express, and you can switch the parts yourself, mailing back the defective part at the company's expense. The only downside is that it takes a couple of weeks for your system to be assembled and shipped. Patience is a virtue, though, and can save you a whole lot of grief later down the road.

Just Push Play

When you go shopping for your new computer, bring a list of the components you need, including the type of video card and sound card, the amount of memory, and the processor speed. If you don't understand computer hardware, bring someone with you who does.

So will your current computer be good enough to at least get you through this book? Unless it's ancient, it'll probably do. In any case, in the next chapter you're about to find out if your system has the right stuff, when you set up your computer for multitrack recording.

The Least You Need to Know

◆ You may be able to get started with recording just by installing the free version of
Pro Tools and plugging a cheap microphone into your computer's sound card.

◆ Most computers purchased in the last few
years should be suitable to get you started
with a home recording studio.

◆ A perfect computer for sound recording
will have a 2GHz Pentium processor and
512MB of RAM, not to mention two
hard drives, one for software and one for
music data.

◆ Although you can start with just about
any sound card, many manufacturers
make sound hardware especially for the
computer-based home studio.

◆ Probably the best place to buy a new
computer is through a mail-order company such as Dell or Gateway.

In This Chapter

◆ Exploring Digidesign's website

◆ Getting your copy of Pro Tools Free

◆ Configuring your system for Pro Tools Free

◆ Installing Pro Tools

Setting Up the Computer

Before you can start following along with the lessons in this book, you need to have some sort of multitrack recording setup. What setup you decide to use depends, as you learned in Chapter 1, on how much you want to spend and how much power and flexibility you think you're going to need. However, to make it easy and inexpensive to get started, and so not to leave anybody behind, this book demonstrates recording concepts using a computer-based home-studio setup running Pro Tools Free. Assuming you already have a decent home computer, you should be able to get set up with Pro Tools Free for next to nothing.

In this chapter, then, you learn how to obtain your own copy of Pro Tools Free and how to get it set up on your computer. I'm assuming that your computer meets the minimum requirements discussed in Chapter 2. Besides that computer system, you're going to need a microphone that you can plug into your computer's sound card. You don't need anything fancy at this point. A $20 microphone from a place like Radio Shack will do just fine.

Getting Pro Tools Free

Because I'm assuming you have a computer, I guess it's also safe to assume that you have an Internet connection. If you don't, it's time you joined the new millennium, anyway! Pro Tools Free is not only free, it's easily downloadable from the Digidesign website. To find your software, point your browser to www.digidesign.com. When you get there, you'll see the web page shown in Figure 3.1.

Figure 3.1   The Digidesign home page.

Near the bottom of the main Digidesign web page, you'll see a link for Pro Tools Free. Give that link a click, and you'll arrive at the page shown in Figure 3.2. Here, you can choose to download the Macintosh or Windows version of the software or to order the software on CD-ROM for $9.95 to cover shipping and handling.

Because I have a Windows system, I'll be going with that version of the program, but Mac users should, of course, download the Macintosh version of Pro Tools Free. The two versions of the software are virtually identical, so you should have little trouble following this book's lessons regardless of your software version.

Notes from the Track Sheet

Currently, Pro Tools Free does not run under Windows XP. If you're running Windows XP, you'll need to install Windows Me, as well. Getting both operating systems set up on your computer is pretty easy to do. First, you need to have at least two partitions on your hard drive. Install Windows Me on drive C and Windows XP on drive D. Windows will automatically set up your hard disk so that you can choose between the operating systems when the computer starts up. Note that Digidesign is currently working on an updated version of Pro Tools Free that will run under Windows XP. That new version might even be available by the time you read this, in which case, this entire note is moot!

Figure 3.2   Here you choose the version of Pro Tools you want.

Assuming you click the link for the Windows version of Pro Tools Free, you'll find yourself at the web page shown in Figure 3.3. Here, you have access to a lot of information about Pro Tools Free. Feel free to poke around a bit and read up on the software. When you're done, click the Download link at the top of the web page shown in Figure 3.3.

You'll now discover that the Digidesign folks want to know a little about the person they're about to give their software to. That is, as shown in Figure 3.4, you need to create a profile on the Digidesign website. Click the Create Profile link, and the page shown in Figure 3.5 pops up.

After entering the required information, click the Create Profile link, which will bring you to the summary page. If everything looks okay, click the Continue link. (If you need to change something in your profile, click the Edit Profile link.) Finally, you can get some downloading done, as shown in Figure 3.6. The two download links on this page enable you to download the Pro Tools Free documentation and the software itself. All told, you're talking about 15MB, which isn't bad at all, although it may take a while for you dial-up modem users to download the files.

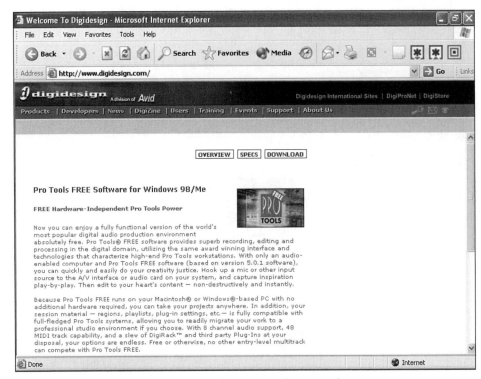

Figure 3.3   The Windows Pro Tools Free web page.

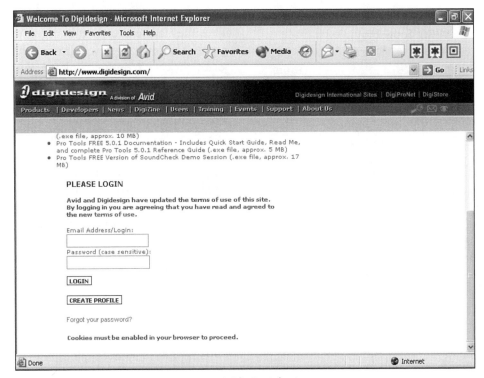

Figure 3.4   Digidesign's login page.

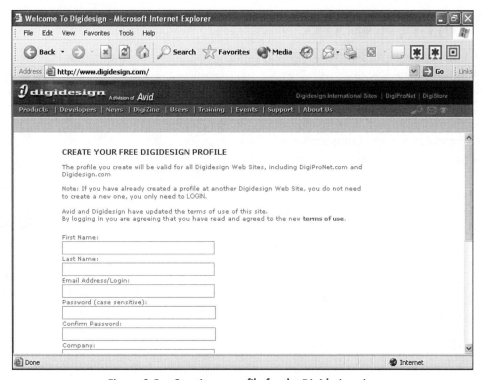

Figure 3.5   Creating a profile for the Digidesign site.

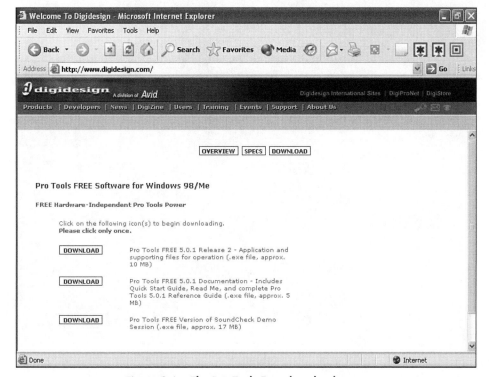

Figure 3.6   The Pro Tools Free download page.

Installing Pro Tools Free

Okay, you've got your downloading done. Make sure you copy the two files—the program and documentation installation files—to a safe storage place (probably a CD-R), so you'll have them if you need them again. Of course, keep copies on your computer, so you can install the software. Before you can install Pro Tools Free, however, you must prepare your system, by disabling Auto Insert for your CD-ROM drive and enabling Direct Memory Access (DMA) for IDE hard drives. (Note that these steps are for Windows users. If you have a Macintosh, follow the similar procedure outlined in the Pro Tools Free documentation you downloaded.) The following steps guide you through these tasks:

1. Select the Control Panel from your Start menu (Figure 3.7).

2. Double-click the System icon, as shown in Figure 3.8.

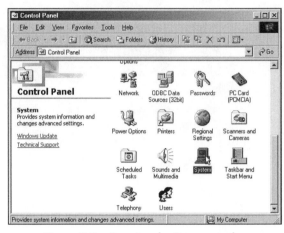

Figure 3.8   Running the System applet.

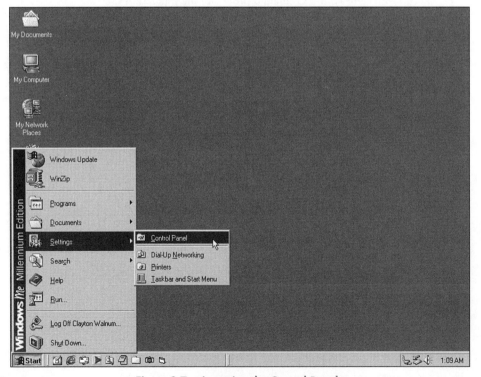

Figure 3.7   Accessing the Control Panel.

3. When the System Properties dialog box appears, select the Device Manager tab (Figure 3.9).

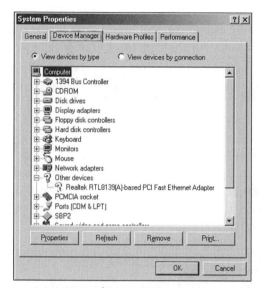

Figure 3.9   The Device Manager page.

4. Find your CD-ROM drive under the CDROM heading (Figure 3.10).

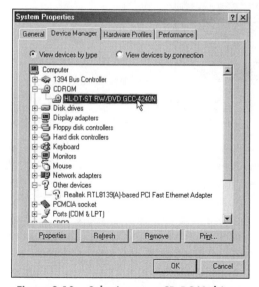

Figure 3.10   Selecting your CD-ROM drive.

5. Double-click the drive's entry to bring up its Properties box (Figure 3.11).

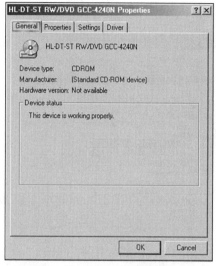

Figure 3.11   The CD-ROM drive's Properties.

6. Select the Settings tab and, if necessary, remove the checkmark from the Auto Insert Notification option (Figure 3.12).

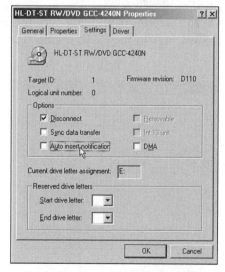

Figure 3.12   Turning off Auto Insert Notification.

7. Click OK to dismiss the CD-ROM drive's Properties dialog box.

8. In the System Properties dialog box, locate any IDE hard drives (Figure 3.13).

Figure 3.13   Locating IDE hard drives.

9. Double-click the drive to bring up its Properties dialog box.

10. On the Settings page, make sure there's a checkmark in the DMA option (Figure 3.14).

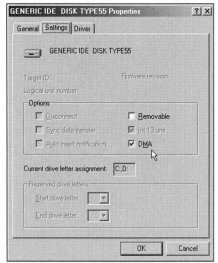

Figure 3.14   Turning on DMA (Direct Memory Access).

11. Click OK to dismiss the hard drive's Properties dialog box, and click OK a second time to dismiss the System Properties dialog box.

That wasn't too bad, was it? Your system is now ready for the Pro Tools Free installation.

Installing Pro Tools Free

Back a little ways in this chapter, you downloaded the Pro Tools Free program and documentation files. Double-click the main Pro Tools Free installation file (not the one for the documentation). When you do, Pro Tools Free's Installation Wizard appears, as shown in Figure 3.15.

Figure 3.15   Starting the Pro Tools installation.

Click the Next button, and you'll arrive at Pro Tools license agreement (Figure 3.16). You have to agree to this contract by clicking the Yes button. When you do, the Pro Tools Free "Read Me" file comes up (Figure 3.17). You should browse through the information in this file to see whether there's anything important you need to know about Pro Tools Free and your system.

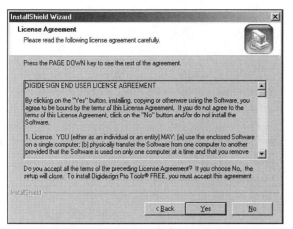

Figure 3.16   The Pro Tools license agreement.

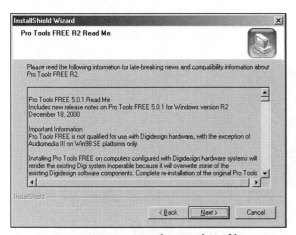

Figure 3.17   Pro Tools's Read Me file.

Finally, you get to the actual installation, which begins when Pro Tools Free asks where you want the program installed on your hard drive, as seen in Figure 3.18. Click the Browse button to choose a location other than the default, or just click Next to accept the default location (recommended for this book).

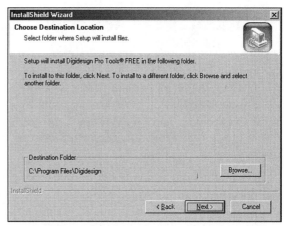

Figure 3.18   Choosing Pro Tools's destination.

After clicking Next, the Installation Wizard asks which components you want to install (Figure 3.19), and you should just click Next, leaving all the components selected. After the installation completes (it goes pretty fast), the Installation Wizard asks you to restart your system. Go ahead and do that, and then meet me at the next paragraph when your system has fully restarted.

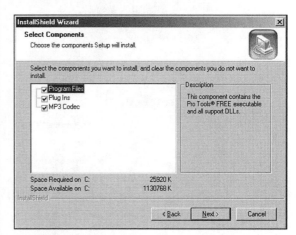

Figure 3.19   The Select Components dialog box.

Finishing the Installation

I know you're anxious to get started with Pro Tools Free, but you still have a couple things to do. First, you need to install the Pro Tools Free documentation, because you're going to want to have it on hand for reference and to learn some of the more advanced stuff we won't get to in this book.

To install the documentation, double-click the documentation file you downloaded. Again, the Installation Wizard pops up. This time, all you have to do is click Next to install the documentation (of which there's quite a bit!).

To find all your newly installed Pro Tools Free goodies, open your Start menu and then open the Programs folder. You should see an icon for Pro Tools Free (Figure 3.20), as well as a folder for Digidesign.

The Digidesign folder contains a Pro Tools folder, which itself contains another Pro Tools Free icon and a Documentation folder. Inside the Documentation folder is, of course, all your Pro Tools Free documentation, as shown in Figure 3.21. (In the figure, the Documentation folder has opened to the left of the Documentation menu. If you have your monitor set for a higher resolution, the Documentation submenu will appear to the right.) You'll also have a Pro Tools Free icon on your desktop, from which you can easily run the program.

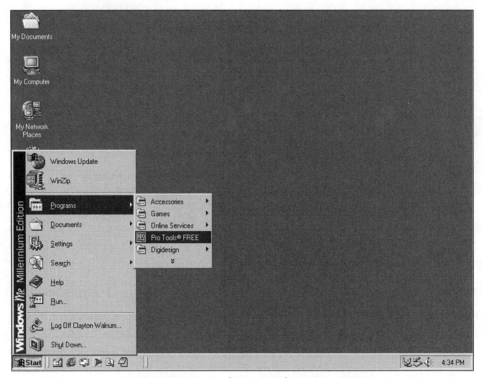

Figure 3.20   Pro Tools Free on the Start menu.

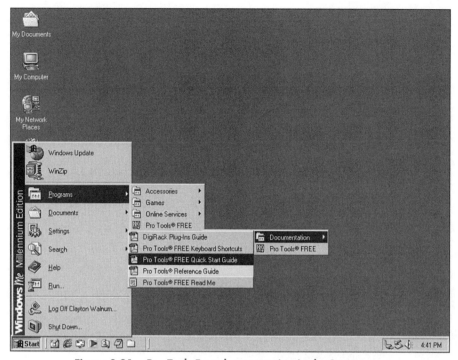

Figure 3.21   Pro Tools Free documentation in the Start menu.

Just Push Play

To read the Pro Tools Free documentation, you must have the latest version of Acrobat Reader installed. If you don't have Acrobat Reader, you can download it free from www.adobe.com. Download the file, and then double-click it to install Acrobat Reader on your system. When the installation is complete, you'll be able to view Pro Tools Free documents by selecting them from the Start menu or from Pro Tools Free's Help menu.

And that's it! You're now ready to explore the fine art of multitrack recording. In the next chapter, you figure out the best way to monitor (listen back to) the recordings you make.

The Least You Need to Know

◆ To find your copy of Pro Tools Free, point your browser to www.digidesign.com.

◆ Pro Tools Free is available for both Macintosh and Windows systems (but, at this writing, not yet Windows XP).

◆ Before you can install Pro Tools Free, you must prepare your system. Windows users must disable Auto Insert for your CD-ROM drive and enable Direct Memory Access (DMA) for IDE hard drives.

◆ To install Pro Tools Free, just double-click the program's icon and follow the installation instructions.

◆ You should also install the Pro Tools Free documentation, which comes in a separate installation file.

◆ To find your newly installed Pro Tools Free, open your Start menu and then open the Programs folder. You should see an icon for Pro Tools Free.

In This Chapter

◆ Deciding between headphones and speakers

◆ Understanding power amplifiers, speakers, and powered speakers

◆ Connecting various types of monitors

◆ Positioning speakers properly

Chapter 4

The Monitoring System

Once you have your recording software or hardware set up, you might think you're ready to get busy. If you're going to be listening to your recordings with headphones, then you probably are. However, although headphones work okay for recording tracks, when it comes time to mix your tracks down to a final stereo recording, headphones don't really cut it. We discuss why later in this chapter, but for now trust me when I say that you should eventually set up a full monitoring system. In this chapter, you learn why this is so important. You also get some suggestions on how to set up your monitoring system.

Headphone vs. Speakers

There's no question that, when it comes to monitoring (listening back to) your recordings, headphones are exceptionally convenient. First, when you're recording your tracks, headphones make it possible to work even in the dead of night, when everyone else is sleeping. (Musicians are born with a special gene that makes them incapable of sleep when there is recording to be done.) If you have the hardware or software needed to plug your instruments directly into your recorder (Figure 4.1)—something you'll learn to do before you're done with this book—you can lay down the most vicious and thunderous guitar-metal tracks without making a peep. Ozzy would be proud!

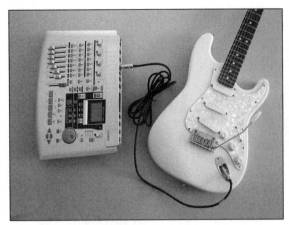

Figure 4.1   Plugging your musical instrument directly into a recorder.

Figure 4.3   These headphones go for about $100, and sound great.

Another plus for headphones is that they are cheap and portable. You can buy a decent pair of headphones for around $50 and a high-quality pair for around $100. That's way cheap compared with the hundreds (or even thousands!) of dollars it costs to set up a good amplifier and speakers. As for portability, would you rather lug around 100 pounds of amplifier-and-speaker stuff or just tuck a pair of headphones into your pocket? If you chose the former, you're either impressingly buff or you have one of those knuckle-dragging fan-roadie-hangers-on people upon whose back you can stack heavy equipment.

Figure 4.2   These headphones, which sound okay, go for about $40.

Figure 4.4   These headphones go for about $300, and sound awesome, although they don't sound three times as good as the $100 headphones.

The problem with headphones—and it's a biggie—is that, no matter how good they are, they do not produce a good facsimile of how your recordings sound when played through speakers. This is because, with headphones, every tiny detail springs out—grinning, drooling, and demanding attention—from the music.

The biggest example of this is what audio people call *stereo separation*, which is how well the left and right channels of a stereo program are isolated from each other. In the case of headphones, because the "speakers" are right up against your ears, the stereo effect is magnified and sounds nothing like a real speaker system. On the other hand, when listening with speakers, sound from the left and right speakers mix together in the room, yielding a more realistic stereo effect.

Figure 4.5   When listening to music in a room, the left and right channels merge a bit, unlike headphones, which exaggerate the sound of a recording, especially the stereo separation.

If you mix your recordings while monitoring with headphones, I guarantee that you will be surprised (and probably not pleasantly) by the results. When played through headphones, such a mix may exhibit any or all of the following problems:

◆ Poor stereo image

◆ Uneven balance between the volume of tracks

◆ Overly subtle effects (for example, too little reverb)

◆ Poor tonal quality

In short, headphones tend to exaggerate everything in your recording, leading you to overcompensate where compensation may not be needed at all. When you're just recording a vocal or guitar part, these problems aren't as critical. By all means, use headphones for recording tracks. In fact, in many cases, such as when overdubbing (adding new tracks to existing

tracks), you have no choice but to use headphones. When it's time to produce your final, mixed product, though, you must have a good-quality monitoring system.

Putting Together Your Monitoring System

Most recording systems supply a headphone output of some sort, but few (maybe even none) come with a power amplifier and speakers. Sure, there are package deals out there where you can buy a recorder along with the monitoring system, but, still, the recorder itself does not come with a built-in power amplifier or speakers. The monitoring system is separate.

To get started, you can just use your home stereo (assuming you have a decent one; I'm not talking about a boom box here) to monitor your recordings. But eventually, you're going to want to get an amplifier and speaker system designed for home-studio use. Why? Because your humble author has money invested in many speaker manufacturers and he wants a good dividend this year. (Uh … did I say that out loud?)

Actually, the reason is that a home stereo system is not designed for use in a studio, because such a system rarely has a flat response to all audible frequencies. If that sounds like Greek to you (or even Dutch, for that matter), think of it this way: Home systems might exaggerate the bass or treble sounds in your recordings. In other words, what you hear coming from the speakers will probably not be the way the recording really sounds.

Amplifiers and speakers designed for studio use are *supposed* to offer flat frequency response, which means that no part of the sound gets exaggerated more than another part. At least, theoretically, that's the way it's supposed to be. The truth is that even different studio monitor setups sound different from each other. There are, after all, a lot of variables, including the room in which you're listening to your music. That is, every room sounds different and every monitoring system has its own peculiarities.

How then can you expect to ever hear exactly what your recordings really sound like? To some extent, you can't; you can only get close. Of course, if you're willing to pay a sound engineer thousands of dollars to build a studio room for you, you can get very close to a perfect listening environment, but all that's for when you release your first gold record. Right now, all you want to do is learn the basics, for heaven's sake!

Connecting to a Computer's Sound Card

Most of you probably aren't ready to invest in special amplifiers and speakers—or in special computer hardware, for that matter. For that reason, we start off with the easiest way to connect your computer to a monitoring system: using your existing computer sound card and connecting it to your home stereo.

To do this, you need a special cable that has a stereo mini-plug on one end and two RCA plugs on the other, as shown in Figure 4.6. You may have even received such a cable with your computer system, because it's not unusual for computer users—especially gamers—to want to connect their sound cards to a quality sound system.

The trouble is that these cables are rarely long enough, usually not more than a few feet. You'll probably need to get an extension cable that has RCA plugs at one end and RCA jacks at the other. You can also get a couple adapters like those shown in Figure 4.7. These adapters have RCA jacks at both ends, so you can plug your computer cable into one end and a regular (and longer, of course) RCA plug cable into the other.

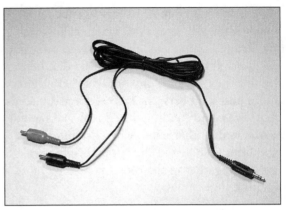

Figure 4.6   The cable you need to connect your computer to a stereo system.

Figure 4.7   Adapters for connecting cables with RCA plugs.

Notes from the Track Sheet

The cable described in this section is typically what you need to connect your computer's sound card to a stereo system. The world, however, overflows with different types of sound cards and stereo systems, and a few of these systems probably have unusual connectors. If the connection described here doesn't work for your system, you need to refer to—*gasp!*—your computer's or sound system's manuals.

Plug the stereo mini-plug into your sound card's line out (see Figure 4.8) and plug the RCA plugs into an appropriate input on the back of your stereo system's receiver, as shown in Figure 4.9. (Note that where you plug into your sound card will probably differ from the jack used in the photo. Sound cards are all different. Ditto on the stereo receiver.)

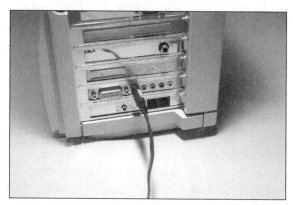

Figure 4.8   Plugging the cable into the computer's sound card.

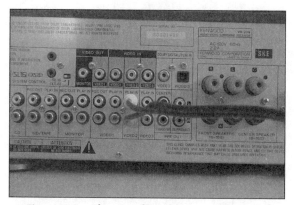

Figure 4.9   Plugging the cable into your stereo system's receiver.

On your stereo receiver, you can use the CD, Tape, or Aux inputs. You can, in fact, use pretty much any audio input except the one labeled Phono (if you even have one), which is designed only for connecting a turntable. (If you're under the age of 18, you might have never even seen a turntable. We old folks used to use turntables to play records, an archaic practice that a friend of mine once described as "dragging a rock through a hunk of plastic.")

Now that you have your cable connected, turn on your stereo system and select the input you used as the sound source. That is, if you connected the cable to the receiver's Aux input, set the receiver to Aux. Set the stereo system to a reasonable volume—we don't want to inflict ear damage on your pets—and then use an audio application on your computer to generate sound. You might, for example, want to load up Windows Media Player to play an MP3 file or a CD. If you did everything right, all your computer's sound should be coming from your stereo system. How cool is that?

Connecting to a Studio Monitoring System

Those of you ready to advance to a more professional setup may be about to purchase—or may have already purchased—a monitoring system designed especially for the home studio. Even if you're not ready to take that step, you probably will be some day, and so you will want to know how to connect it and how it all works. Somehow, I ended up charged with the job of guiding you through this process. (Oh yeah, I signed a contract.) Luckily, it's a job I like as much as getting a back massage from Sarah Michelle Gellar. All together now: *Buf-FY, Buf-FY, Buf-FY!*

Unfortunately, unlike computer sound cards and home stereos, studio monitoring systems don't exhibit a lot of similarities from one to the next. That is, I can only generally guide you in the connection process. For the details, you need to refer to (*gasp!*) the manuals. Such systems do, however, work pretty much the same way, with the main difference being the type of cables used to connect it all up.

Two General Types of Monitoring Systems

When you go shopping for your studio monitoring system, you'll confront two main choices:

◆ A system with separate power amplifier and speakers

◆ A system with powered speakers

The first type of system—the one with a power amplifier and separate speakers—is a lot like what you have with a component stereo system. The amplifier is roughly equivalent to your stereo system's receiver, and the speakers are roughly (okay, exactly) equivalent to your stereo system's speakers. Figure 4.10 shows a power amplifier with a set of speakers, both of which are specially designed for studio work.

Figure 4.10   The power amplifier and speakers as separate components.

The second monitoring system listed is the one that's the best choice for a small home studio, for reasons you'll soon learn about. In this type of system, the power amplifiers are built right in to the speakers themselves, rather than being a separate component.

Figure 4.11   Powered speakers have the amplifier built right in.

Using Separate Amplifier and Speakers

First, let's take a look at a monitoring system using a separate amplifier and speakers. The big difference between your stereo system's receiver and a power amplifier is that the power amplifier has only two inputs (usually, anyway), one each for the left and right channels of a stereo audio signal, as shown in Figure 4.12.

Figure 4.12   Power amplifiers need only two inputs, one for each stereo channel. They also have two outputs for the speakers.

Also on the back of the power amplifier are the speaker outputs, which Figure 4.12 also shows. Although there may be several types of speaker connections, usually you connect only one set of speakers to the amplifier. Note that each speaker requires two wires for a total of four connections.

Because a power amplifier has only two inputs, it doesn't need all the buttons and switches that your stereo receiver has. Generally a power amplifier has three controls: a power switch, volume for the left channel, and volume for the right channel, as shown in Figure 4.13.

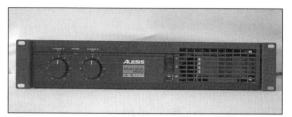

Figure 4.13   Power amplifiers usually have only three main controls.

The speakers in this type of system are much like the ones in your stereo system, except that they are designed to provide a flat frequency response. Obviously, the more you pay for these speakers, the better they are at approaching a flat frequency response, but never forget that the room in which you use them—and even where you place them in the room—has a lot to do with how they sound. We cover that sticky problem a little later in this chapter. For now, just know that the monitor speakers are very similar to the ones you probably have with your stereo system and so should hold little mystery, even to a home-studio novice.

How to connect your component monitoring system to your studio hardware depends a lot on the connectors available on each of the components. In the simplest setup—a computer with a standard sound card—you need a cable with a stereo mini-plug on one end. The plugs you need at the other end depend on your power amplifier, but you'll probably need standard ¼-inch phono plugs, such as those used on the end of a guitar cable. Figure 4.14 shows such a cable.

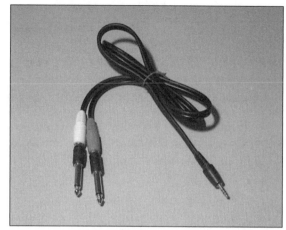

Figure 4.14   The cable for connecting a computer's sound card to a power amplifier's inputs.

The cable in Figure 4.14 is actually the same type of cable you'd use to connect your computer's sound card to your home stereo. That is, the cable itself has a stereo mini-plug on one end and two RCA plugs on the other. The cable in the photo, though, has two adapters attached to the RCA ends that change those plugs to standard ¼-inch plugs. Figure 4.15 shows what the adapters look like when they're detached from the cable.

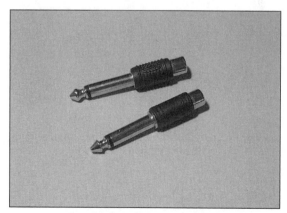

Figure 4.15   Adapters for changing an RCA plug to a standard ¼-inch plug.

Figure 4.16 shows the general connections you need to make for a more sophisticated system, by which I mean one that is computer based with a special sound card or one that is noncomputer based, such as an all-in-one studio workstation. The connections go like this:

◆ **Connection 1:** From the recorder's or sound card's left monitor output to the power amplifier's left input

◆ **Connection 2:** From the recorder's or sound card's right monitor output to the power amplifier's right input

◆ **Connection 3:** From the power amplifier's left output to the left speaker

◆ **Connection 4:** From the power amplifier's right output to the right speaker

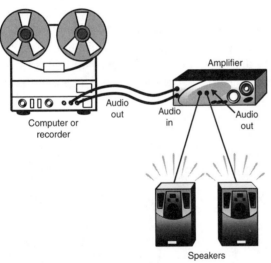

Figure 4.16 Connecting up a typical monitoring system in a home studio.

Just Push Play _____

You don't have to connect your computer to a monitoring system if you don't want to. For most of the examples in this book, you can just plug a decent set of headphones into your computer's headphone jack. If you're not using a computer (for example, you already have some other type of multitrack recorder), whatever you *are* using almost certainly has a headphone jack, too.

Using Powered Monitor Speakers

Now, let's take a look at a monitoring system using powered speakers. As I mentioned previously, this type of monitoring system's amplifiers are built right in to the speakers. These monitors offer many advantages. The most obvious is their compactness and portability. Also, because the amplifiers and speakers are combined, you have fewer cables to connect. The most important advantage, however, is that the speakers and amplifiers are perfectly matched for each other, which means you get the best sound quality the monitoring system is capable of producing.

Connecting powered monitors is a lot easier than connecting separate amplifier and speaker components. In fact, you need make only two connections, as shown in Figure 4.17. The connections go like this:

◆ **Connection 1:** From the recorder's or sound card's left monitor output to the powered speaker's left input

◆ **Connection 2:** From the recorder's or sound card's right monitor output to the powered speaker's right input

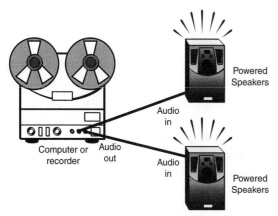

Figure 4.17   Connecting powered speakers in a home studio.

Notes from the Track Sheet

These days, many monitoring systems have both analog and digital audio inputs. Analog inputs are the same type you have on your home stereo system. Digital inputs must be connected, with special cables, from digital outputs on your recorder. If you don't know what any of this digital stuff means, stick the analog connections for now.

Positioning the Speakers

At this point, we could get into a whole ball of wax about stuff like sound treatments for your studio room, where you end up sticking foam (among other things) all over the walls. We're just starting off here, though, so we'll leave all that nonsense for the experts. To get started with your monitoring system, you only need to know, first, whether it works, and, second, where to put your speakers.

The speakers typically used in home-studio setups are called *near-field monitors,* because you set them up close to where you work, rather than mount them on the wall. The distances between properly positioned near-field monitors and your head (that's where your ears are, dummy) should form an equilateral triangle. Figure 4.18 shows what the setup should look like. I probably should also mention that the speakers should be about five or six feet apart. If I don't, I just know someone will try to cram his or her head between two speakers a foot apart.

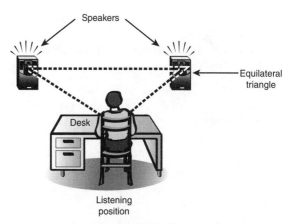

Figure 4.18   Positioning speakers in a home studio.

Just Push Play

Poorly positioned speakers yield bad stuff such as songs with unbalanced stereo separation. For example, if one speaker is closer to a side wall than the other, the wall reflections will shift the stereo image to one side. Then, when you mix your music, you'll overcompensate by placing too much sound on the other side, and … well, you can see the kind of mess you could get into. In short, make sure that your left and right speakers have exactly the same environment.

I should also mention that near-field monitors should not be placed in corners or even near walls. That is, you need to have a reasonable amount of space all around the speakers. If you're setting up your studio system on a desk, for example, the desk should be a couple of feet away from all walls. If you don't have a lot of space on your desk, you can invest in a set of speaker stands. In any case, the speakers' height should be the same height as your ears when you're sitting at your studio desk. I'm assuming, of course, that your ears are on the sides of your head!

Notes from the Track Sheet

You may wonder why you shouldn't place your near-field monitors near walls or (especially) in corners. Such a placement causes an increase in the speakers' low-frequency response. That is, the speakers will produce more bass than they should, pretty much killing any chance of your getting a flat sound.

Testing the Monitoring System

Okay, you're now ready to see whether you can actually get sound out of your monitoring system. To do that, you're going to have to turn on your recorder (computer or otherwise) and the power amplifier. *Wait!* Not yet! First, an important hint: Turn on the power amplifier last and do so with the volume turned down. If you don't, you may get some nasty thumps and pops when you turn other stuff on. In most cases, these unexpected sounds are just annoying, but a good loud thump can damage your speakers, not to mention scare the bodily fluids from anyone standing nearby.

Got everything turned on? Cool. If you're using your computer as your studio centerpiece, use any software you like to produce sound. I suggest playing a CD or MP3 file with Windows Media Player or some other music software. If you're using another type of recorder, such as an all-in-one workstation, you need to play a recording on that. How you do that depends on the system you have, but generally, you load a song and press the play button. Most compact studio systems come with a sample song you can use for this purpose. If you're stumped at this point, you have to refer to the (*gasp!*) manual.

And that should take care of your monitoring system. Whether you're sticking with headphones for the time being or have set up full-featured studio monitors, you're ready to move on to the next chapter, where you learn about some odds and ends you need before you can start recording.

The Least You Need to Know

◆ Headphones are exceptionally convenient, making it possible to work even in the dead of night.

◆ The problem with headphones is that, no matter how good they are, they do not reproduce how your recordings sound when played through speakers.

◆ To start off, you can use your home stereo to monitor your recordings, but eventually, you should get an amplifier and speaker system designed for home-studio use.

◆ Amplifiers and speakers designed for studio use are supposed to offer flat frequency response, which means that no part of the sound gets exaggerated more than another part.

◆ Home-studio monitoring systems come in two main types: separate components (separate power amplifier and speakers) and powered speakers (all-in-one amplifier and speakers).

◆ The distances between properly positioned near-field speakers and your head should form an equilateral triangle, with the speakers about five feet apart and on the same level as your ears.

In This Chapter

- ◆ Understanding dynamic and condenser microphones
- ◆ Discovering microphone response patterns and frequency response
- ◆ Getting stands and cables
- ◆ Shopping for other helpful studio equipment

Chapter 5

Microphones, Cables, and Other Helpful Goodies

You're close to starting recording, but no home studio is complete without microphones, not to mention the various cables you need to connect them. Most studios also equip themselves with useful things like cable adapters, microphone stands, and other stuff that makes recording simpler and easier. In this chapter, you examine some items that no home studio can do without.

Microphones

When it comes to microphones, you've got a whole heap of choices, and if you make the wrong choice, you won't like the results. Some types of microphones are better suited to some tasks then others, and even different brands of the same types of microphones sound different from each other. Luckily, certain microphones—and one in particular—have proven themselves over the years and are almost essential for both home and professional studios.

But we won't get into that yet. First, let's examine the different types of microphones you might run into, either in a studio or when shopping in your local music store. I don't bother with the many weird or special-purpose microphones out there. Instead, we stick with the types of microphones that are most useful for your home studio.

Dynamic and Condenser Microphones

Probably the most common type, dynamic microphones, are especially handy, because they require no power supply. In fact, dynamic microphones are a lot like speakers, except they gather sound rather than give it off. Dynamic microphones are also very sturdy and can take a lot of sound pressure from loud instruments, such as drums or electric guitar.

Notes from the Track Sheet

Both speakers and microphones are called *transducers*, and you can actually use a speaker as a microphone, although it won't do the best job. Theoretically, you can use a microphone as a speaker, but I wouldn't advise it. Microphones aren't designed to take the power that gets delivered to a speaker, so plugging a microphone into a speaker output is sure to fry the mic faster than a strip of bacon in an industrial-strength microwave.

The most popular dynamic microphone in the world is the Shure SM57 (Figure 5.1), and if you can afford only one microphone, this is the one to get, because it works well across a whole spectrum of uses from vocals to drums. I doubt there's a single studio in the world that doesn't have a set of these babies. The good news is that SM57s are actually inexpensive, with a street price of around $85. Can you believe it?

Condenser microphones are among the best (and most expensive) microphones you can buy. They tend to be much more sensitive to high frequencies than dynamic microphones. However, they are also more sensitive to sudden loud sounds—so much so, in fact, that they are often a bad choice for instruments like drums (unless they are placed away from the set). Instead, condenser mics are better used for vocals and acoustic instruments.

Figure 5.1   The Shure SM57 is a standard studio workhorse.

One disadvantage of condenser microphones is that they require a power source. Many types can run on batteries, which is convenient, but usually condenser mics get plugged into a mixer or other device that provides *phantom power*. Phantom power is a voltage that the mixer (or other device) delivers to the microphone right through the microphone's cable. Strangely, a condenser microphone's cable is no different from any other microphone cable, which is, I guess, why they refer to the voltage as phantom power. It seems to come from nowhere!

Just Push Play

If a condenser microphone doesn't seem to work, first make sure it's turned on. Many condenser mics have on/off switches right on the mic. If the switch is on, but the mic still doesn't work, check for phantom power from the device into which the mic is plugged. Often, phantom power must be turned on with a switch somewhere. If the mic uses a battery as a power supply, make sure the battery is still good. If none of this gets the mic working, try using a different cable. If that fails too, you've probably got a dead mic, dude! You didn't try to use it as a speaker, did you?

Audio-Technica makes some excellent condenser microphones, perfect for recording things like vocals and acoustic guitar. Figure 5.2, for example, shows the AT4040. The prices on these microphones tend to the high side though (at least, when compared to dynamic mics), with the AT4040 going around $400. If you think that's expensive, go to your local pro studio and ask how much their favorite vocal mic costs. They'll probably tell you something like $5,000!

I should also note that condenser mics come with small or large diaphragms. The large-diaphragm mics tend to have more uses and so are a good bet for your home studio. Want a couple of usage examples? You'll often see large-diaphragm condenser mics used for vocals or for recording acoustic guitar, whereas engineers sometimes use small-diaphragm condenser mics for drum overheads. However, no one will stop you from using a large-diaphram mic as a drum overhead. (They finally caught that guy.)

Figure 5.2   The Audio-Technica AT4040 condenser microphone.

Just Push Play

Two other good, inexpensive condenser mics are the Audio Technica 4033, which goes for around $260, and the Rode NT-1, which can be had for less than $200.

Microphone Response Patterns

Now we've managed to divide microphones into two categories: dynamic and condenser. Another characteristic that separates one mic from another is the *response pattern*, which specifies the direction from which the microphone picks up sound. Some microphones can "hear" only sound that comes from mostly in front, whereas others can pick up sound from all around them. Others, of course, fall somewhere in the middle between these two extremes.

A *cardioid* mic (also called a *unidirectional* mic) is the one that picks up sound from mostly in front. Figure 3.3 shows such a microphone as if you were looking down on top of it. The heart-shape pattern around the mic shows the directions from which it receives sound. Cardioid mics are the first choice for mic'ing single sound sources, such as a vocalist, a guitar amp, or a drum.

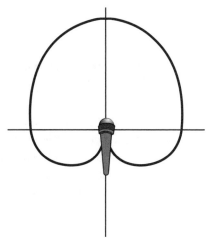

Figure 5.3   The response pattern for a cardioid microphone.

Notes from the Track Sheet

There are a couple of variations on the cardioid response pattern: hypercardioid and supercardioid. We don't get into such special-purpose microphones here, though. It's enough just to know they exist.

The opposite of a cardioid mic is an *omnidirectional* mic, which picks up sound from everywhere. Figure 5.4 shows its response pattern. You might want to use such a microphone to record a group of background singers, who would arrange themselves in a circle around the microphone.

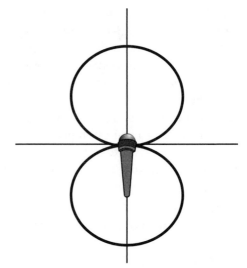

Figure 5.5   The response pattern for a bidirectional microphone.

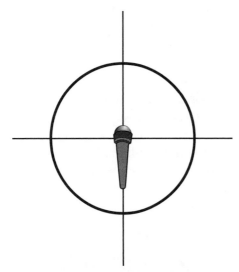

Figure 5.4   The response pattern for an omnidirectional microphone.

In the middle between the cardioid and omnidirectional mics is the *bidirectional* mic (also known as a "figure-eight" mic), which picks up sound from the front and rear, but not from the sides. Figure 5.5 shows the response pattern for a bidirectional mic. You might use such a microphone to record two singers facing each other.

Microphone Frequency Response

Believe it or not, you still need to know a few more things about microphones—*frequency response*, for example. Every sound you hear is made up of one or more frequencies. Bass notes are way down in the low frequencies, whereas cymbals are way up in the high frequencies. To make the highest-quality recording possible, a microphone must capture sound in all the frequencies contained in the sound being recorded.

While some microphones are designed to work better with different ranges of frequencies, in a small home studio, you want to get as much use from your microphones as possible. After all, unless you just came into a big inheritance or won the lottery (hold on, let me check my ticket), you're not going to want to buy a slew of special-purpose microphones. Nope, you're going to want one or more all-purpose, do-everything-as-best-as-possible-for-the-money mics.

Generally, you need to look for microphones with the broadest frequency response. Moreover, you want this frequency response to be similar at all frequencies—in other words, a *flat* frequency response. (Remember when we talked about flat frequency response for speakers back in Chapter 4? The same holds true for microphones.) Luckily, in these high-tech days, most quality, general-purpose microphones boast a broad and flat frequency response. Specifically, most good microphones have a mostly flat response from 50Hz all the way up to 15KHz.

The Shure SM57, for example, is a great, general-purpose microphone because it has a frequency response from 40Hz to 15KHz, with a little extra brightness in the 5Khz to 7KHz range. (In other words, its frequency response is generally flat, except that it responds slightly better to frequencies between 5KHz and 7KHz.) This extra brightness translates to a little more presence in the recorded sound.

As for special-purpose microphones, a good mic for low-frequency sound sources such as a bass guitar or especially a kick drum is always a good investment. In my studio, I have an AKG D112 (Figure 5.6) that I use on kick drums. This mic is specially designed to take the abuse dealt out by a high-energy sound source like a kick drum. Moreover, the D112 has a frequency response from 20Hz to 17KHz. Notice that this mic "goes lower" than does the venerable SM57. You pay for that privilege, though, since the D112 goes for about $200, more than twice the cost of an SM57.

Figure 5.6   The AKG D112 kick-drum and bass-guitar microphone.

Impedance

The last thing to consider with a microphone is its *impedance*. Impedance is to alternating current what resistance is to direct current. If that means nothing to you, that's okay. Just know that there are both low-impedance (low-Z) and high-impedance (high-Z) microphones and that they are not interchangeable. That is, a high-impedance mic must be plugged into a high-impedance input, and … you guessed it … a low-impedance mic must be plugged into a low-impedance input. This is called *impedance matching.*

Most microphones used in studios—including home studios—are low impedance. This is because low-impedance microphones can be connected to longer cables, and they generate less line noise. High-impedance mics must be connected to shorter cables, but can produce higher-level output. (As with everything in this universe of ours, compromise is the rule of the studio.)

You can quickly tell whether a microphone is high or low impedance (usually, anyway) by looking at its plug. Generally, if you need a cable with an XLR plug (Figure 5.7), the microphone is low impedance. If you need a cable with a ¼-inch plug (Figure 5.8), such as that on a guitar cord, the microphone is high impedance.

Of course, exceptions abound. You don't expect all this to be easy, do you? You might, for example, run into a high-impedance microphone with an ⅛-inch mini-plug rather than a ¼-inch phono plug (Figure 5.9). You often see this type of microphone used with small portable devices or with home computers. In fact, if you're not going to be investing in any fancy equipment before you finish this book, you'll want at least a microphone like the one shown in Figure 5.9, because it'll plug directly into your computer's sound card, as shown in Figure 5.10. (Such a microphone may have even come with your computer, although it may look different from the one in the figure.)

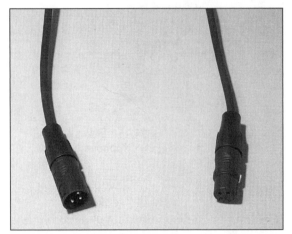

Figure 5.7   Most low-impedance microphones require cables with three-prong XLR plugs.

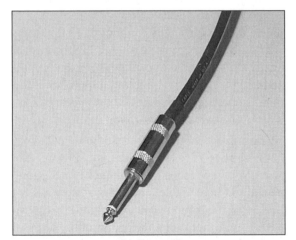

Figure 5.8   Most high-impedance microphones require cables with ¼-inch phono plugs.

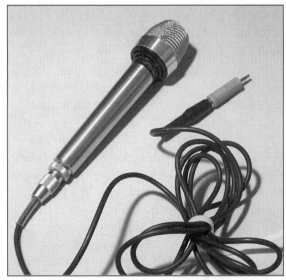

Figure 5.9   A high-impedance microphone with a ⅛-inch mini-plug.

Figure 5.10   A high-impedance microphone plugged into a laptop computer's sound card.

Other Goodies

So that's about it for microphones—at least, that's all you need to know to get started. I could write an entire book on microphones alone, but we want to start recording sometime before the next millennium, right? But first, let's look at some handy extras with which you might want to equip your studio, starting with microphone adapters.

You can—in spite of my previous phrase "not interchangeable"—connect a low-impedance mic to a high-impedance input and vice versa. Well, sort of, anyway. You first have to plug the mic into something called a *line-matching transformer*. This isn't as big a deal as it may sound. For example, a line-matching transformer that enables you to plug a low-impedance mic into a high-impedance line input is just a small adapter and costs as little as $12 (Figure 5.11). One end of this adapter accepts a three-prong XLR plug, and, as you can see in the figure, the end that gets plugged into the high-impedance input is a ¼-inch phono plug.

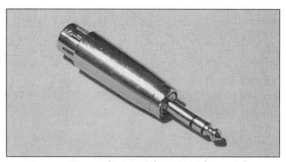

Figure 5.11   A line-matching transformer that enables you to plug a low-impedance mic into a high-impedance line input.

These impedance adapters are very handy to have around. Sooner or later, you're going to want to use a line input for a microphone. Why? Because reasonably priced home recording hardware often provides only one or two low-impedance mic inputs, with the rest of the inputs being high-impedance line inputs. This is how they keep prices down. (Line inputs don't need mic preamps, for one thing.) Figure 5.12, for example, shows the inputs on the back of a Tascam 788 Digital Portastudio. Not a single low-impedance microphone input! The Tascam 788 does, however, come with two line-matching transformers. Figure 5.13 shows a low-impedance microphone plugged into the Tascam 788 using one of these transformers.

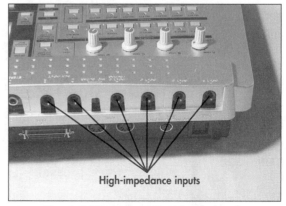

High-impedance inputs

Figure 5.12   To keep its price down, the Tascam 788 provides only high-impedance inputs.

Figure 5.13   A low-impedance microphone plugged into the Tascam 788 using a line-matching transformer.

More important than impedance matchers, however, are microphone cables, which rarely come with microphones. (Don't ask me why. It's just one of those things we musicians have to put up with, along with the drunks at bars and the high cost of purple hair dye.) You can spend very little or a whole lot for a microphone cable. In most cases, you'll see a 20-foot cable for about $15, but the professional studios may have cables that cost $100 or more—and that's just for one! You and me, we'll stick with the cheaper ones (Figure 5.14).

Figure 5.14   Most microphones require a cable that you have to buy separately.

You're also going to want microphone stands, which, like everything else in this business, come in several varieties. The most useful in a home studio, though, is the boom stand (Figure 5.15), which is a conventional mic stand with an extra, adjustable arm. Using these stands, you can get a mic positioned just about anywhere you want. An average price for a boom stand is $45, but you can pay more for the sturdier varieties.

Figure 5.15   A typical microphone boom stand.

Another handy type of mic stand for the studio is the mini-stand shown in Figure 5.16. These "shorty" stands are great for mic'ing kick drums and small guitar amplifiers. You can also use them to sneak microphones into unobtrusive places and so monitor private conversations. I won't, however, be doing that again—at least not until after my court date.

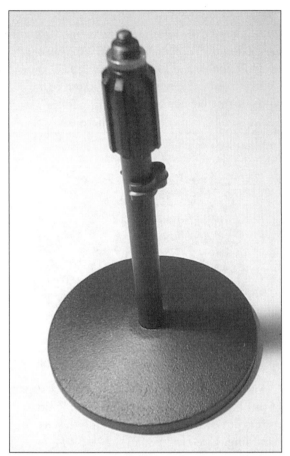

Figure 5.16   **A typical microphone mini-stand.**

Figure 5.17   **A special microphone holder that clips right onto a drum.**

If you're going to be mic'ing real drums, boom stands are almost a must. But even better are the special mic holders that clip right to the side of the drum (Figure 5.17). These handy doo-dads get all those bulky stands out of your way. More important, they get everything out of the way of the drummer. Believe me when I say that drummers just *love* to stand up suddenly and knock over your carefully placed boom stands. They swear it's always an accident, but I don't know …

Impedance transformers aren't the only types of adapters that come in handy. You're going to run into plenty of times when the input you need requires one type of plug and your only available cable has another. For example, RCA plugs and ¼-inch plugs show up all the time for line inputs and outputs. What if you need to plug into a RCA jack but only have a cable with a ¼-inch plug? Luckily, there's always an inexpensive adapter for the job. Figure 5.18 shows a selection of adapters from my "tackle" box.

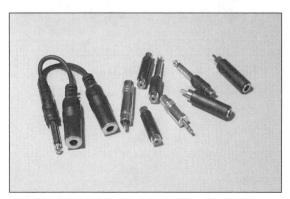

Figure 5.18   **An assortment of handy adapters.**

And If You Want to Splurge ...

Sooner or later, you'll need most of the stuff we discussed so far in this chapter. There are, however, many other cool devices that simplify and supercharge your recording tasks. If you lack a place where you can wail on your guitar, one device that you need is an amp simulator. These electronic marvels reproduce the sound of classic guitar-amp setups without making a sound. Your guitar plugs into the simulator, and then the simulator plugs into your recorder. You can listen to the results through your monitors or with headphones.

Figure 5.19 shows the Line 6 POD that I have in my studio. This puppy not only lets me choose between a bunch of different amps, but also includes guitar effects and even a guitar tuner. Amp simulators like the POD go for around $300. Several other manufacturers make similar products.

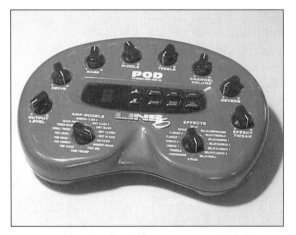

Figure 5.19   The Line 6 POD amp simulator.

For bass guitar, I use a SansAmp Bass Driver DI (Figure 5.20), which lets me plug a bass guitar directly into my recorder. The various controls enable me to get whatever bass sound I want, from a clean, warm jazz sound to a wildly distorted punk sound.

Figure 5.20   The SansAmp Bass Driver DI.

And this brings us to the end of the first part of this book. That means that the preliminary stuff is out of the way, and it's time to start recording. *Woo-hoo!*

The Least You Need to Know

◆ Dynamic microphones are especially handy, because they require no power supply and tend to be very sturdy.

◆ Condenser microphones are among the best (and most expensive) microphones you can buy.

◆ A microphone's response pattern specifies the direction from which the microphone picks up sound.

◆ Generally, you need microphones with the broadest and flattest frequency response. Most good microphones have a mostly flat response from 50Hz all the way up to 15KHz.

◆ A high-impedance mic must be plugged into a high-impedance input, and a low-impedance mic must be plugged into a low-impedance input—unless you use an impedance-matching transformer.

◆ Most microphones used in studios are low impedance, because low-impedance microphones can be connected to longer cables, and they generate less line noise.

In This Part

Part 2

The Recording Process

Now that you have your home studio set up, you can start recording. In this part of the book, you learn all the basic techniques of getting your song from your head and into a multitrack recording project. Along the way, you help produce a real song project called "Pro Tools Blues." You work on this song all through the rest of the book.

First, you learn about multitrack recorders and how they work. You then discover how to record the basic tracks upon which you will build your final song. If you're a solo artist, this may mean recording a click track or drums first. If you're recording a full band, you'll probably record the rhythm instruments—at least drums and bass—first.

Once you have your basic tracks recorded, it's time to add additional instruments, including instrumental solos and vocals. You learn to add these tracks one at a time using a process called overdubbing. Along the way, you also learn to patch up mistakes in performances, as well as how to use effects like compression to ensure well-recorded tracks.

In This Chapter

◆ Discovering the history of the multitrack recorder

◆ Starting a new Pro Tools Free session

◆ Adding tracks to a session

◆ Recording tracks

◆ Saving a Pro Tools Free session

Chapter 6

Recording and the Multitrack Recorder

The heart of every studio—whether a modest setup in your basement or a full-featured, professional business—is the multitrack recorder. This is the machine that takes dozens of microphone and instrument inputs and records them onto some sort of media. This media could be magnetic tape (same as the stuff in your cassettes and VCR tapes, only about 2 inches wide and 100 times more expensive), the surface of a computer's hard drive (as it will be in our case), or sometimes even a special memory card, such as the SmartMedia cards used in many pocket recorders and cameras.

But no matter what form a multitrack recorder and its media takes, they all have one thing in common: to get them to work requires a doctorate degree in rocket science, the support of at least three members of the U.S. Congress, and a uniform comprised of purple jeans and a pink, ruffled shirt. No, wait! What they have in common is that in order to record music, you have to know, at least generally, how they work. As for the purple jeans and the ruffled shirt, I won't say anything if you don't.

Where Did the Multitrack Recorder Come From?

The multitrack recorder was invented by a well-known guitarist named Les Paul. Les Paul was, in fact, such a talented and well-known guitarist, that one of the most-used and highest-quality guitars in the world is named after him. In a big way, we have Les to thank for being able to march down to the local music store and buy a CD that sounds so darn awesome.

Why? Because the multitrack recorder gives a record producer an immense amount of control over how the final product sounds.

Notes from the Track Sheet

Besides Les Paul, two other people deserve a heap of credit for the existence of modern recorded sound. The first is Alexander Graham Bell, who invented the telephone, and in so doing, discovered how to convert sound into an electrical signal. The other person to thank is Thomas Edison, who figured out how to record sound in a way that could be played back. How about a few gusty *Huzzahs!* for these fine chaps?

Way back in the day—say in the 1940s—all of the hit songs (and all the junky ones, too) were recorded using a single microphone stuck in the middle of the room, as shown in Figure 6.1. The band would play its parts while the singer did the best job he could manage, all of them knowing that if they made a mistake, the entire recording would have to be abandoned and redone.

Figure 6.1   In the early days of recording, an entire group would be recorded with a single microphone.

For example, if the drummer was playing too loudly and drowning out the singer, the recording engineer would have to reposition the microphone and the group would have to try the recording again. Talk about a pain in the butt! Getting all of the instruments balanced was a long and difficult system of trial and error.

As an attempt to solve this recording problem, Les Paul (remember him from a few paragraphs ago?) came up with the idea of *overdubbing*, which is the process of adding new sound to an existing recording. Les Paul first recorded a guitar part on a phonographic disc machine, as shown in Figure 6.2.

First-generation guitar part A

Figure 6.2   Recording the first guitar part onto a disc.

Then he would play back the first recording, while playing a second part on his guitar, recording both parts onto another disc, as shown in Figure 6.3.

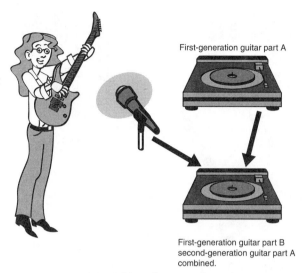

First-generation guitar part A

First-generation guitar part B
second-generation guitar part A
combined.

Figure 6.3   Adding the second guitar part.

Theoretically, this overdubbing could go on and on until the artist has stacked dozens of instruments onto a single recording. The problem is that every time a sound is rerecorded, it loses quality. So when Les Paul played the first guitar part (we'll call it part A) onto disc, he had a first-generation recording of part A. However, after he made his second recording (part B), by combining his first recording with a new guitar performance, the new disc had a first-generation part B, but a second-generation part A. So part A did not sound as good as part B. Dig?

When using this type of overdubbing, with each generation the sound quality gets worse. If Les Paul then took the combined recording of parts A and B, and added a part C, he would have a recording consisting of the following:

◆ A first-generation recording of part C

◆ A second-generation recording of part B

◆ A third-generation recording of part A

The solution, of course, is to give up music all together and let somebody else figure out all this nonsense. But maybe a better solution is to record each instrument or vocal onto its own disc and then, when it's time to listen to the final product—play all the disks at exactly the same time. Unfortunately, this solution is not only impractical, but downright impossible. Or is it?

Enter Magnetic Tape

Around this time, people were getting away from recording directly onto a disc and were instead using tape recorders with magnetic tape. There are at least three things that are cool about magnetic tape:

◆ It can be used again and again.

◆ It can be divided into tracks.

◆ It can be fun to unravel all over a room.

The first item in the list isn't important to our discussion of multitrack recorders, although it is important when it comes to saving money in a recording session. The third item I just put in because a list of less than three points looks dumb (and, anyway, it *is* fun to make a mess with magnetic tape; you can even use it to make cool wigs). The second item in the list is the one that made the first multitrack recorders possible.

Imagine, for example, that you want to record a saxophone solo onto a tape recorder. So you plug a microphone into the recorder, start the recorder, and play your saxophone. In the case of the early tape recorders, you would have only one track to work with. So you'd end up with a saxophone on one track of tape, as shown in Figure 6.4.

Saxophone

Figure 6.4   A saxophone solo recorded onto a single-track tape.

Now, it's very cool that your saxophone solo is preserved for the ages, so that your kids and grandkids can all hear the great job you did and wonder why you didn't earn millions playing your instrument. But how much better would that saxophone have sounded with a guitar backup?

To add a guitar to your recording, you need another track. By having another track, you can have a first-generation recording of both the saxophone and the guitar, rather than the second-generation saxophone you'd end up with if you tried to overdub the guitar as previously described.

You could use two tape recorders, recording the saxophone on one recorder and the guitar on the other (Figure 6.5). Then, if you have superhuman timing (ready, set, *GO!*), you could start playback on both machines at the exact same time so that the two tracks—the sax and the guitar—played back perfectly synchronized. I probably should have put the word "superhuman" in italics, because unless you fit into that category, it's going to take a whole lot of luck to get the recordings to synchronize!

But here's an idea, how about combining the two machines into one? I don't mean to take a sledge hammer and beat them into a single pile of rubble—although I can't tell you how many times during a bad recording session I've been tempted to do exactly that. What I mean is, what if you had a recorder that could record two tracks, side by side, onto a single tape, as shown in Figure 6.6?

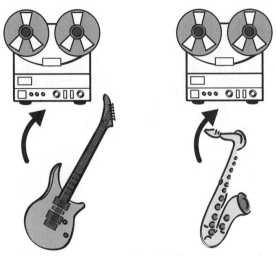

Figure 6.5   Two recorders enable you to record two instruments on separate tracks, but, when it's time to play your recording back, good luck starting both machines at the exact same time.

Figure 6.6   A single recorder with two tracks, one for the sax and one for the guitar, makes it easy to synchronize the two instruments at playback.

The single tape would be divided into two distinct horizontal areas, track 1 and track 2. You could then record your saxophone onto track 1 and your guitar onto track 2 (Figure 6.7). Moreover, playback would be a snap because both pieces of the song would be on one tape and could be played back with the flick of a single switch—presumably the Play switch on the recorder and not the Start switch on your blender. Now you have an honest-to-goodness, awesomely audacious, multitrack recorder.

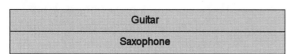

| Guitar |
| Saxophone |

Figure 6.7 A two-track tape on which has been recorded a saxophone and a guitar.

One of the first multitrack machines used to record professional music was a four-track recorder. As you can now guess, that meant that the tape the machine recorded onto was divided into four distinct areas, enabling the session's producer and engineer to record four different musical performances onto the same tape, and then play them back perfectly synchronized. Figure 6.8 shows a representation of how the tape was divided.

| Drums |
| Bass |
| Guitar |
| Vocals |

Figure 6.8   A four-track tape containing four synchronized musical performances.

Of course, the tape on which the performances were recorded wasn't itty-bitty like those shown in the figures. What was used (and still sometimes is) was huge reels of tape many hundreds of feet long. In fact, even today, it's not uncommon to need 30 inches of tape for each second of recording time.

One very powerful feature of a multitrack recorder is that not all of the tracks have to be recorded at the same time. Consider a drums, bass, guitar, and vocals example. If you have the talent, you can record the drums first onto one track. Then, rewind the tape and record the bass part while listening to the drum part you just finished. Ditto for the guitar and vocal parts. Now you're a one-person band!

The first widely used professional multitrack recorders relied on four-track tape, and you might be amazed at the extraordinary albums that were made on these machines. Probably the most famous is The Beatles' masterpiece *Sgt. Pepper's Lonely Hearts Club Band,* which was not only a landmark album in terms of its musical content, but also in the way it was produced. Get a copy of this album, put it on your stereo, slap on some headphones, and listen. All the while, keep reminding yourself that *this album was recorded on four-track machines!*

Luckily, The Beatles had the brilliant George Martin as their producer. Martin (*Sir* Martin to us peasants) had the technical savvy and the extraordinary creativeness needed to work miracles with four-track recorders. He used every trick in the book, true, but at the heart of *Sgt. Pepper's Lonely Hearts Club Band* is a four-track recorder.

Once the use of multitrack recorders in studios became commonplace, the race was on. It wasn't long before there were 8-track recorders, 16-track recorders, and so on. Today, it's common for a studio to handle 72 tracks or more.

Starting a Pro Tools Free Session

All that brings us to our first experiment in modern recording. Even though Pro Tools Free runs on your computer, it still uses the idea of tracks to organize your recordings. To see what

I mean, run Pro Tools Free. When the program is up on the screen, your first step is to create a new session, which creates on your hard disk the files you need to start recording. Follow these steps to create your first session and set up four tracks for recording (if you have any trouble, you can find the complete session in the Chapter06\Test directory of this book's CD-ROM):

1. Select New Session from the File menu (Figure 6.9). The Name the Session dialog box appears.

2. Make sure the 24-bit option is selected (Figure 6.10).

3. Change the file name to Test, and click Save. Pro Tools Free creates a set of files for the session, and the Edit window appears, as shown in Figure 6.11.

4. Double-click the Edit window's title bar. The window fills Pro Tools's workspace (Figure 6.12).

5. Select the New Track command from the File menu (Figure 6.13). The New Track dialog box appears (Figure 6.14).

6. In the Create box, type the number **4,** and then click the Create button. Four new audio tracks appear in the Edit window, as shown in Figure 6.15.

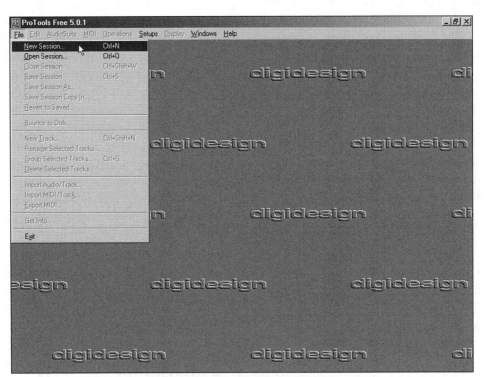

Figure 6.9   Creating a new session.

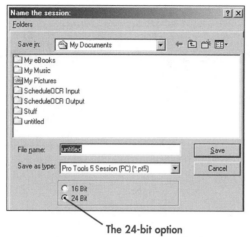

The 24-bit option

Figure 6.10   Selecting the 24-bit box.

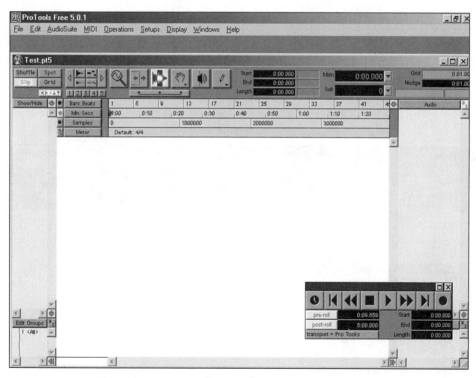

Figure 6.11   Pro Tools Free after starting a new session.

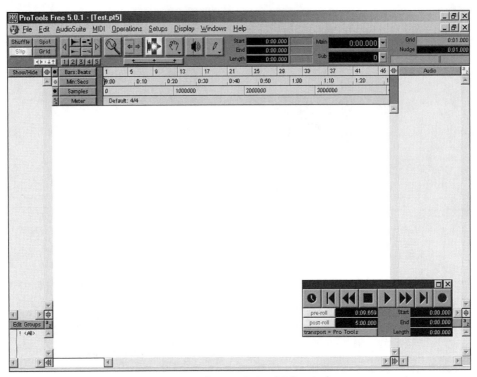

Figure 6.12   The maximized Edit window.

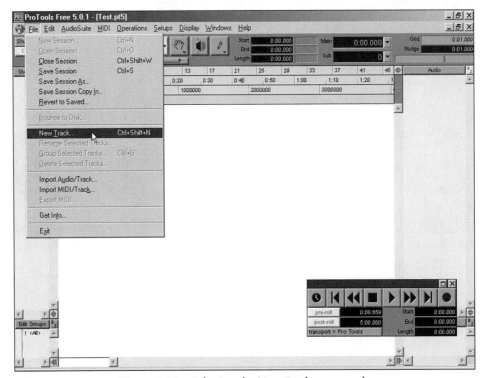

Figure 6.13   Selecting the New Track command.

Figure 6.14   The New Track dialog box.

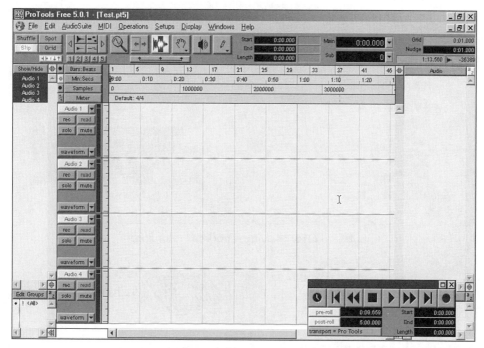

Figure 6.15   The new four-track session ready to go.

Recording a Track

As you can see now in Pro Tools's window, the four tracks you're about to use for your first recording are similar to the tracks you saw back in Figure 6.8. That is, the tracks are four horizontal strips onto which you can record four different sounds. Ready to try it out? First, plug a microphone into your computer's sound card (or whatever you're using).

Now, you have to tell Pro Tools Free which tracks you want to record. You do this by clicking the Record button for each track you want. If you look to the left of each of the tracks, you'll see a group of four buttons marked Rec, Read, Solo, and Mute. Click the Rec button on the first track to ready it for recording (Figure 6.16). When you do, the button's background turns white and the button's text turns red, letting you know that it's ready for recording.

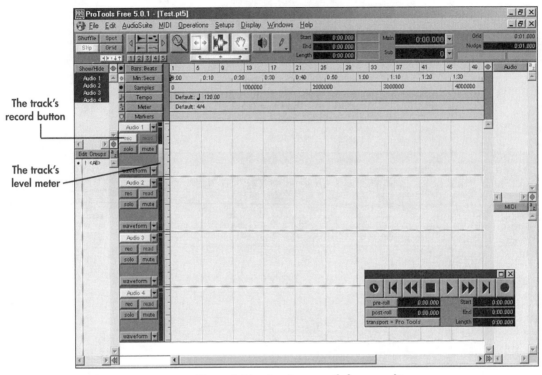

The track's record button

The track's level meter

Figure 6.16   Arming a track for recording.

Just to the right of the buttons, you should see a vertical green bar that's jumping up and down a bit. This is the track's level meter, which tells you the level of the sound being routed to the track. When recording a track, you should record with as high a level as possible, without pushing the level meter "into the red," a condition that often causes digital clipping. Believe me, digital clipping is a nasty sound that you want to avoid.

When you talk into your microphone, you should see the level changing in the level meter. If you don't, either you're talking into your computer's mouse instead of the microphone, or your computer isn't set up properly for the microphone. You need to refer to your computer system's and sound card's manual to correct this situation.

Just Push Play

Generally, you can think of a track's level as its volume. But technically, level and volume are different things. Our ears perceive volume as an average of changing levels over time. The level meters in Pro Tools show you the level at any instant in time, which is why they change so much. It's true, though, that as you make what you're recording louder, the higher the level meter goes. When the top of the meter turns red, you need to turn down the volume of the track's input.

If you're running Windows, you probably want to look at the recording section of the sound mixer to make sure that the microphone input is turned on and that its volume is up.

Following is a general procedure for doing that. But keep in mind that how your mixer looks varies with the type of sound card you have and which version of Windows you're running—which is why you may need to refer to your manuals. That goes for you Mac people, too.

1. Go to the Start menu and open Control Panel from the Settings menu, as shown in Figure 6.17.

2. Double-click the Sounds and Multimedia icon (Figure 6.18). The Sounds and Multimedia Properties dialog box opens.

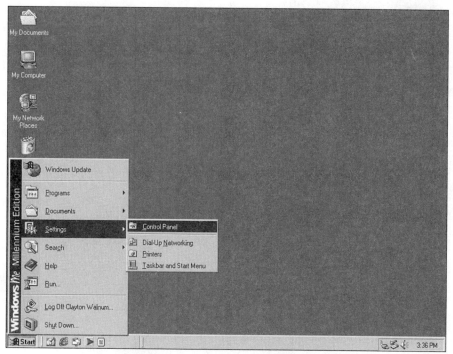

Figure 6.17   Opening the Control Panel.

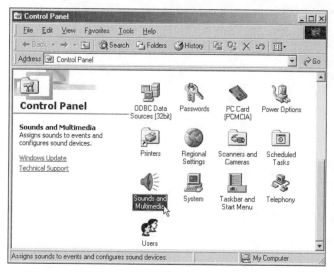

Figure 6.18   Clicking the Sounds and Multimedia icon.

3. Click the Audio tab. Your current audio settings appear in the dialog box, as shown in Figure 6.19.

Figure 6.19 The audio settings.

4. In the Sound Recording box, click the Volume button. The Recording Control dialog box appears, as shown in Figure 6.20.

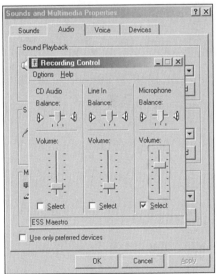

Figure 6.20 The Sound Recording dialog box.

5. In the Microphone section, make sure the Select box is checked and that the volume level is up.

Placing the Recorder into Record Mode

Just because the track is now ready to record doesn't mean that it *is* recording. In fact, except for the level meter, the track is doing nothing right now. To record, you must put the recorder into record mode, which you do by clicking the red button (actually, the dot on the button is so darkly red that it looks almost black) in the Transport window, as shown in Figure 6.21. That button will then begin to blink. To start your recording, click the Play button, also in the Transport window. If you've ever recorded a cassette or some other kind of tape, these controls should be familiar.

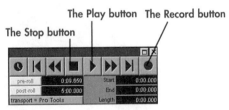

Figure 6.21 The Transport window.

Recording at Last!

When you click the Play button, the recording on track 1 begins. Go ahead and talk into the microphone, or just tap on it. It doesn't matter what you do, as long as you record some sound. How can you tell whether you're recording sound? The sound's waveform appears in the track that's recording. After 15 or 20 seconds, click the Stop button in the Transport window. Recording stops, with the track's complete waveform appearing in its strip, as shown in Figure 6.22.

Track's waveform

File name of audio file

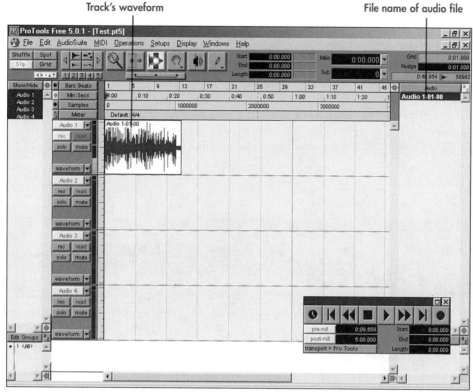

Figure 6.22   The newly recorded track.

The name of the audio file that holds the waveform's data appears in the Audio Regions List to the right of the tracks. Pro Tools stored this file on your computer's hard disk, in the Session's folder.

Now that you're done recording the track, click the track's Rec button to take it out of record mode. This ensures that you won't accidentally start recording over what you just did—not that, at this point, it's likely to be much of a loss! Now, click the Play button in the Transport window. Your recording starts to play back. Cool, huh?

Recording a Second Track

Now, let's add a second recording to your session. In other words, let's overdub a new

instrument. In this case, the instrument is whatever you're doing with the microphone, but it could be anything: guitar, drums, saxophone, belches. I bet you can figure out how to record the second track, but just so you're sure, here are the steps:

1. Click the second track's Record button.
2. Press the Record button in the Transport window.
3. Press Play in the Transport window.
4. Use the microphone to record some sound.
5. Press the Stop button in the Transport window.
6. Click the track's Rec button to turn off its record mode.

You should now see a waveform in the second track, as shown in Figure 6.23. Press the Play button in the Transport window, and both tracks play back at the same time. You can continue to add tracks to your recording, up until the maximum of eight allowed by Pro Tools Free. (The LE version of Pro Tools allows 32 tracks.) For example, if you were to record two more tracks, you'd see a screen something like that shown in Figure 6.24.

And there you go, your first multitrack recording. To close Pro Tools Free, click the × in the upper-right corner. Pro Tools Free then asks if you want to save your changes (Figure 6.25). Click the Save button, and Pro Tools Free saves your entire session to your computer's hard disk, from which you can reload it at anytime.

Figure 6.23   The newly recorded second track.

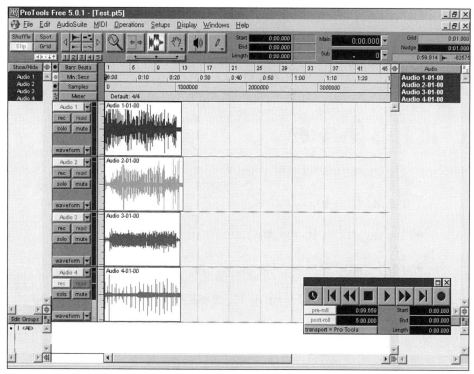

Figure 6.24   After recording four tracks.

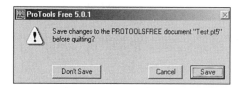

Figure 6.25   Saving your session.

You should now have a pretty good idea of what a multitrack recorder is and how it works. If you don't, either I've failed as your author or you fell asleep somewhere between the chapter's title and this sentence. In any case, in the next chapter, we get busy recording some music for real.

The Least You Need to Know

◆ Multitrack recorders can record multiple instruments on separate tracks, with all tracks being of first-generation quality.

◆ With a multitrack recorder, tracks can be recorded one at a time, rather than all at once.

◆ Even though Pro Tools Free runs on your computer, it still uses the idea of tracks to organize your recordings.

◆ To enable a track for recording, click its Record button (labeled Rec).

◆ Each track has a level meter that shows the level of the track's input.

◆ Every time you record, Pro Tools Free creates audio files on your disk.

In This Chapter

- ◆ Creating a recording plan
- ◆ Recording live drums
- ◆ Using drum loops and drum machines
- ◆ Importing audio files
- ◆ Creating stereo sound from mono tracks

Chapter 7

Recording the Basic Tracks

In the previous chapter, you learned to create a new Pro Tools Free session, as well as how to record on multiple tracks. We were just fooling around then, though, learning to use Pro Tools Free, but not recording anything of value (unless you got ambitious).

Obviously, recording real music—that is, something other than microphone taps or other test noises—takes a lot more effort and skill. First, you need to play an instrument or two. Next, you're going to need to know a little more about Pro Tools Free. In this chapter, we cover all this territory.

Planning Your Song

The first step (besides writing or choosing a song to record) is to figure out exactly how you're going to go about the task. If you don't want to play yourself into a corner (mixed metaphors, anyone?), you're going to need a plan. For example, here are some questions you need to ponder:

◆ What instruments do you intend to use in the recording?

◆ Which instruments should you record first?

◆ Should you record a bunch of tracks at the same time (assuming you have a band) or is it better to record each part separately?

◆ How many vocal parts will there be?

◆ Are you going to record real drums, use loops, or use a drum machine?

◆ How are you going to cram everything into the available tracks?

The exact questions depend to some extent on the song you want to record. The previous list is just an example of what you might want to ask yourself and by no means represents all the questions that can arise.

Let's assume that you're going to record a blues-y number with the following tracks:

◆ Drums

◆ Rhythm guitar 1

◆ Rhythm guitar 2

◆ Lead guitar

◆ Bass guitar

◆ Lead vocal

◆ Harmony vocal

If each instrument gets a track of its own, you're up to seven tracks, which is fine because Pro Tools Free gives you eight tracks to work with. However …

Recording Live Drums

One snafu is recording drums. Drums are usually recorded in stereo, which requires two tracks, not just one. Live drums, moreover, are usually recorded with five or more microphones, each microphone going to its own track.

For example, let's take a basic drum kit (Figure 7.1) comprised of a kick drum, a snare drum, a high-hat, two mounted tom-toms, a floor tom, a ride cymbal, and a crash cymbal. Even a small set like this has a lot of stuff to mic.

Figure 7.1   A basic drum kit.

Placing Drum Microphones

You can place microphones on this drum set in a number of ways. Here's a list of the most likely choices:

◆ Place a single microphone where it picks up the best balance of drum sounds. Route the mic to a single track.

◆ Place two microphones where they pick up the best stereo image of the drums. Route the mics to two different tracks.

◆ Place two microphones where they pick up the best stereo image of the drums. Then add microphones to the kick drum and the snare drum. Route all mics to just two tracks.

◆ Place two microphones where they pick up the best stereo image of the drums. Then add microphones to the kick drum and the snare drum. Route each mic to its own track.

◆ Place a microphone on every piece of the drum kit, and route all the microphones to only two tracks.

◆ Place a microphone on every piece of the drum kit, and route each microphone to its own track. Premix all the tracks down to one or two before recording other instruments.

◆ Place a microphone on every piece of the drum kit, and route each microphone to its own track. Keep all tracks separate (that is, no premixing).

Notes from the Track Sheet

In case you can't tell by that humongous list, drums are a pain in the patootie to record. The only thing tougher to record is the sound of my wife admitting I'm right, because, of course, that never happens. Dig this: Often in a pro studio, the engineer spends the entire day setting up drum mics and getting the best drum sound. That's an entire 10-hour day at like $250 or more an hour!

These drum mic'ing methods start with the simplest and the least expensive in terms of the number of tracks to record (leaving more room for other instruments). Going down the list, each method generally requires more mics or more tracks—not to mention an increased risk of your having a nervous breakdown. But the results further down the list also result in a "higher-quality" recording.

I put "higher-quality" in quotes because the method you use depends a lot on the results you need. That is, "high-quality" is a relative term. If you're recording a quick booking demo for your punk band, the first few drum-mic'ing methods may be just fine. On the other hand, if you're recording a CD to sell online or at your shows, you're probably going to want to use a method further down the list.

Getting the Microphone into Pro Tools Free

The bottom line is that the more microphones and tracks you use to record the drum kit, the more control you have over the drums when it comes time to mix all your tracks down to stereo. But (there's always a *but*, isn't there?), if you're really lucky and skillful, you could choose a method somewhere in the middle of the list and still get as good a drum track as you would have got using the "best" method. Remember: The Beatles' *Sgt. Pepper's Lonely Hearts Club Band* was recorded on four-track machines, which means that there weren't too many tracks to dedicate to drums.

One problem that arises, however, is how to get a bunch of microphones routed to different tracks in Pro Tools Free. If you're using the stripped down setup with just your computer's sound card, you're pretty much out of luck. To get multiple microphones connected to Pro Tools, you need to pick up some extra hardware, maybe the Pro Tools Digi 001 system, which comes with a special external sound card (Figure 7.2) for your computer, as well as a much more powerful version of Pro Tools. (Up to 32 tracks, dude!)

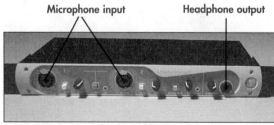

Figure 7.2 The Digi 001 interface for your computer.

The Digi 001 system, which goes for about $750, provides a number of different inputs and outputs, both on the front and back of the interface. The front features two microphone inputs, whereas the back (Figure 7.3) provides a bunch of other inputs and outputs. All you have to do is plug your microphones into the interface, and then use Pro Tools to route them to the tracks you want, as shown in Figure 7.4.

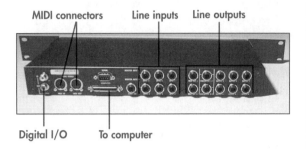

Figure 7.3   A back view of the Digi 001.

For maximum flexibility, though, you need additional microphone preamps, which are where you can plug in low-impedance microphones. The Presonus DigiMAX LT (Figure 7.5) works great with the Digi 001, giving you eight additional microphone inputs. The knobs on the front control the level of the microphone inputs on the back (Figure 7.6). However, this shiny piece of metal goes for around $800. Combine that with the $800 for a Digi 001 system, and you're starting to spend some bucks. Luckily, all this fancy hardware is beyond the scope of this book, so you can put your wallet away for now.

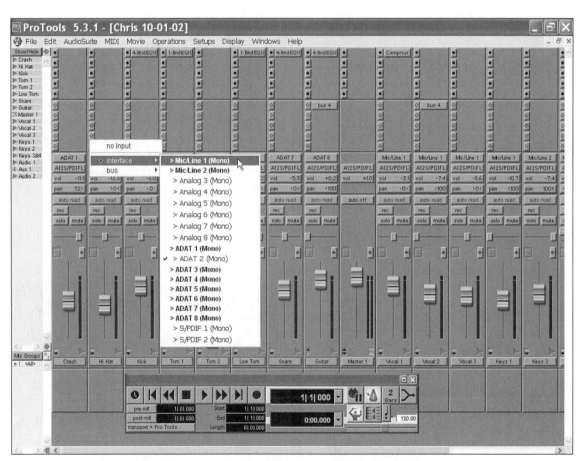

Figure 7.4   Routing inputs to tracks in Pro Tools LE.

Figure 7.5   Additional hardware can provide more microphone inputs.

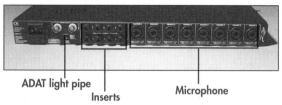

ADAT light pipe

Inserts

Microphone

Figure 7.6   A rear view of the DigiMAX LT.

Just Push Play

The rear of the DigiMAX LT features some I/O types that you may not be familiar with. The coolest one is the ADAT light pipe. This connector enables you to send all eight microphone channels to the Digi 001 across a tiny optical cable. The jacks labeled Inserts, on the other hand, actually handle input and output with a single jack. Using one of these jacks you can plug in an effect box or other type of processor (most likely a compressor) for each microphone input.

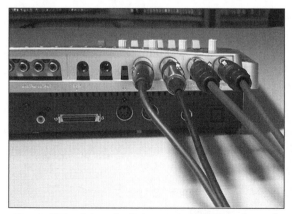

Figure 7.7   A bunch of drum microphones plugged into an all-in-one workstation.

Audio Shoehorns

You know, I just reread my previous comment about audio shoehorns, and I heard this loud voice in my head. That either means that my medication has worn off or that this book's tech editor, my good buddy Dan, left a note for me. Yep, there's a note, all right. (Thank heavens it wasn't the medication. I'm getting tired of holding conversations with lamps.) Dan has just reminded me that audio shoehorns do indeed exist. They're handy things called mini-mixers. I even own one and used to use it all the time with my drum machine.

If you take a gander at Figure 7.8, you can see the drum machine, and if you look forward to Chapter 13 and search out Figure 13.22 (it's easy to find; it's right after Figure 13.21), you'll see the type of mini-mixer Dan reminded me of. You can get one of these versatile mini-mixers for less than $100.

I'm about to tell you how you can use a mini-mixer and a drum machine (or even live drums) to get great stereo drum recordings without eating up a lot of tracks. First, though, you need to have a drum machine with at least four assignable outputs (Figure 7.8). Because my machine has four, we'll go with that. Here's how the deed is done:

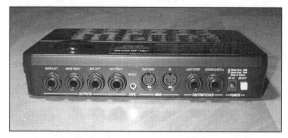

Figure 7.8 Four outputs on a drum machine.

1. Assign all drums sounds except the kick and snare drums to the drum machine's first two outputs, which are the normal left and right outputs. (Obviously, you need to refer to your drum machine's manual.)

2. Assign the kick drum sound to the drum machine's third output and the snare drum sound to the fourth output. With a real drum set, this setup would be the equivalent of using two overhead mics along with a kick-drum mic and a snare-drum mic.

3. Route the four outputs from the drum machine into a mini-mixer. Figure 7.9 illustrates these connections.

Figure 7.9   Connecting the drum machine's outputs to the mini-mixer.

4. Route the stereo outputs of the mini-mixer to two inputs on the recorder, giving you stereo drum tracks. Figure 7.10 shows this connection.

Figure 7.10   Connecting the mini-mixer to the recorder.

Using a mini-mixer combined with a drum machine can be extremely powerful technique. You need to notice, however, a couple of things about the setup. First, you may wonder why four cables come out from the drum machine, but only three go into the mixer. The answer is that the third input strip on the mixer is actually a stereo input. That is, it's two inputs in one. So the cable running between the mixer and the drum machine has a stereo plug on one end (the end that goes into the mixer) and two mono plugs on the drum machine end. Figure 7.11 shows this special cable when it's unplugged from everything.

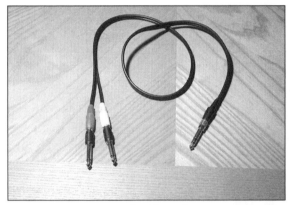

Figure 7.11   A special cable with a stereo plug on one end and two mono plugs on the other.

Just Push Play

You can also use a mini-mixer to record a live drum kit. In that case, you plug the drum mics into the mini-mixer and the mixer's stereo output into your recorder or even into yet another mixer. This is a cheap way to add inputs to just about any recording setup.

Another thing to notice is that, thanks to the mini-mixer, you have complete and handy control over the volumes of the kick, snare, and stereo drum tracks, yet you're still only using two tracks on your recorder.

But there's more. This particular drum machine (an Alesis SR16) enables you to assign any drum sound on the machine to any of the machine's four outputs. Moreover, each drum sound has its own volume control. (You access the volumes in the small LCD screen.) What all this means is that, even though you're tying up only two tracks on your recorder, you have full control over every drum sound, just as if you were mic-ing each drum separately and running those mics into a big-mongo mixer. That's so cool that it's downright nuts!

Just Push Play

You can do even more with the drum-machine recording technique we just discussed. Because you're running your drum machine into a mixer, you can use EQ, compression, or any other effect you want on each of the four mixer tracks. In fact, the ability to process the kick and snare drums individually is one of the main reasons you'd want to use the mini-mixer.

Forget All This Live Drum Nonsense! Loops Rule!

If you're feeling like maybe you should leave drum recording to the more experienced at this point, your instincts are probably right. I would never discourage you from experimenting with recording live drums—especially if your band's drummer can kick your butt. But you do need a lot of equipment that you probably don't have yet. Because this is a book for newbies, why not go a simpler route?

For my own solo recording projects, I often use *drum loops*. Drum loops are professionally recorded drum parts that you can string together in various ways to construct a drum track for your song. Using drum loops relieves you from having to own a dozen good microphones.

Moreover, drum loops ensure (assuming that you bought a quality library) that the drums sound professionally recorded. Best of all, you get high-quality drums that require only two tracks for stereo or just one track for mono. Drum-loop libraries cost between $50 and many hundreds of dollars, but even the cheaper ones usually sound good.

Another way to go is a drum machine. These electronic marvels go for between $200 and $500 on average, and can provide convincing, if somewhat mechanical, drum parts for your songs. A drum-machine recording isn't likely to fool a discerning ear, but with a little cleverness, you can create fairly realistic drum parts. Figure 7.12 shows the Alesis SR-16 drum machine, which has a street price of about $200.

Figure 7.12   The Alesis SR-16 drum machine.

To record tracks with a drum machine, you first program the drums on the machine. Then you plug the machine's outputs into your recorder's inputs, start the recorder going, and then press Play on the drum machine. The drum machine plays the drum sounds you programmed, and the recorder records the drums onto one or more tracks, depending on how you set up the recorder. Figure 7.13 shows a drum machine plugged into an all-in-one workstation.

Figure 7.13 **Recording drums from a drum machine.**

Drum machine outputs   Recorder inputs

In case you haven't noticed, I strongly suggest that the first tracks you record include drums. This is because you need some sort of steady beat upon which to build your song. Some people start by recording a *click track*, which is little more than a steady beat, maybe from a metronome, recorded onto one track of the session. The musician then uses the click track as a meter reference for the entire project. When you record your drum tracks first, they function not only as your song's drums, but also as a click track.

Pro Tools and Drum Loops

Creating a drum track from drum loops with Pro Tools Free is pretty easy, thanks to the powerful Pro Tools digital audio editor. The first step is to listen to the loops, of course, and find the ones that will work best for your song. Once you find the loops you want to use, copy them to your hard drive (assuming the loops are WAV files), where you can access them easily from inside Pro Tools.

On this book's disk, you can find a set of drum loops I created especially for this chapter. You can find them in the Chapter07 folder.

Because commercial drum-loop libraries are copyrighted, I couldn't include anything like that on the disc. Instead, I created the drum loops using a drum machine. I could have used a real drummer, but ... well ... I'm lazy. Let's see how you might use such loops with Pro Tools Free. Start up Pro Tools Free, and follow along with these steps:

1. Start a new 24-bit session named ProToolsBlues, as shown in Figure 7.14.

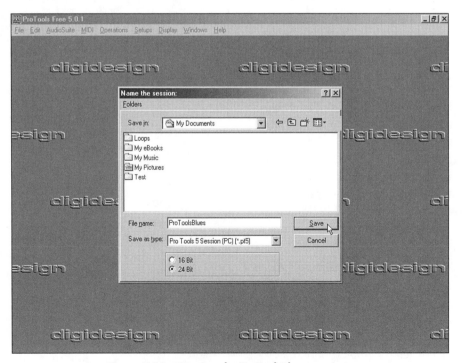

Figure 7.14 **Starting the ProToolsBlues session.**

2. Add two audio tracks to the session, as shown in Figure 7.15.

3. Click the Audio button above the Audio Regions List (Figure 7.16). The Audio Regions menu appears.

4. Select the Convert and Import Audio command, as shown in Figure 7.17. The Convert & Import dialog box appears.

5. Use the Look In box to find the folder in which you stored the drum loops, as shown in Figure 7.18.

6. Select one of the drum-loop files, and then click the Import Files button (Figure 7.19). The file appears in the box on the right side of the dialog box.

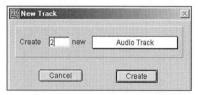

Figure 7.15 Adding two tracks for the drums.

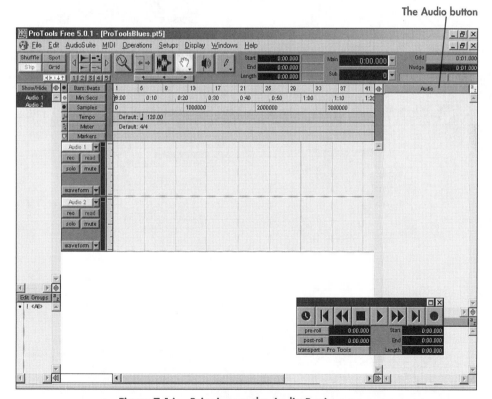

Figure 7.16 Bringing up the Audio Regions menu.

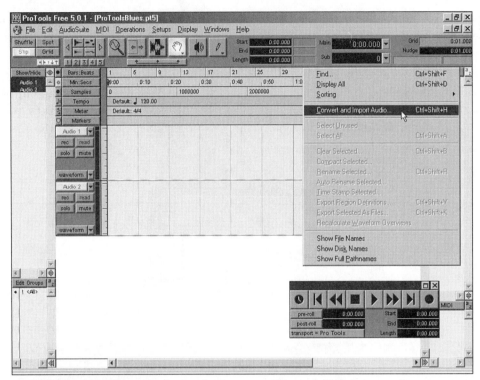

Figure 7.17   Selecting the Convert and Import Audio command.

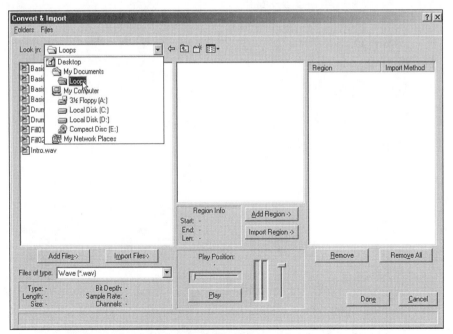

Figure 7.18   Selecting the folder that contains the drum loops.

Click loop to select it

Import Files button

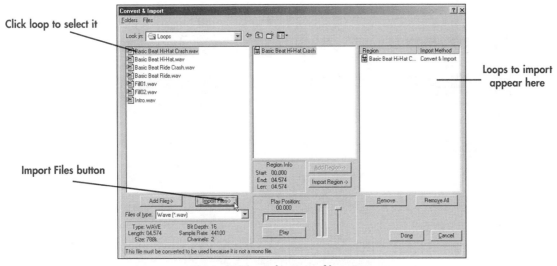

Loops to import appear here

Figure 7.19   Selecting a file to import.

7. Use the same method to add the remaining loops to the box on the right side. When you're done, you should have seven drum-loop files in the box on the right, as shown in Figure 7.20.

8. Click the Done button in the lower-right corner to process the loops. Pro Tools asks for the folder in which to store the imported loops (Figure 7.21).

9. Click the Use Current Folder button. Pro Tools Free processes the loops and adds them to the Audio Regions List (Figure 7.22).

To see the loop file list better, you can increase the Audio Regions List's width. To do this, use your mouse to drag the double-arrow button, as shown in Figure 7.22. Now you have an easily accessible pool of audio files from which to build your drum tracks. Click somewhere in the Edit window to deselect the tracks in the Audio Regions List.

Wanna see something cool? Click one of the loop files, and drag it into track 1 (Figure 7.23). Presto! You just added the drum loop to the

ProToolsBlues project. Cool, eh? Now, try this: If your mouse cursor still looks like a hand, use it to drag the loop around in the track. If the mouse cursor doesn't look like a hand, click the hand button shown in the figure. This button selects the Grabber tool. As long as you have the hand cursor, you can drag the loop anywhere you want in the track.

You don't know this, but you're currently using the Slip edit mode. You can tell by the fact that the Slip button (Figure 7.23) in the upper-left is active. To assemble a drum track from loops, though, you need a more precise way of dragging the loops. Pro Tools Free has just the thing, called Shuffle mode.

Click the Shuffle button, which is located above the Slip button, and then drag the loop again in the track. Now, the only place it'll go is at the very beginning of the track. Choose another loop from the list, and drag it into the track. The loop automatically positions itself seamlessly after the first one (Figure 7.24). You could also place this loop in front of the first one or even between other loops if you have more in the track.

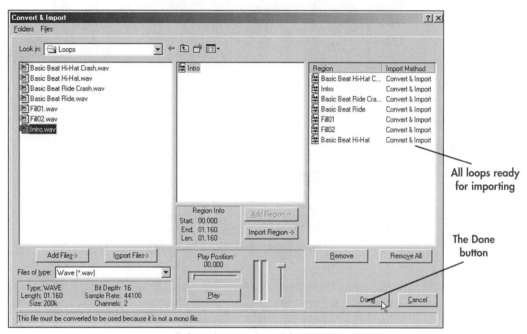

Figure 7.20   All drum loops selected for importing.

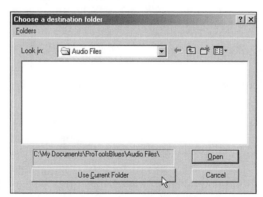

Figure 7.21   Selecting a folder for the
imported loops.

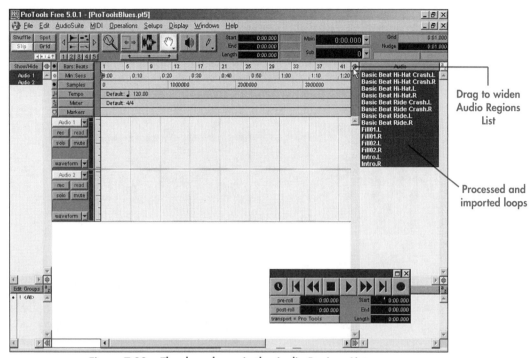

Figure 7.22   The drum loops in the Audio Regions List.

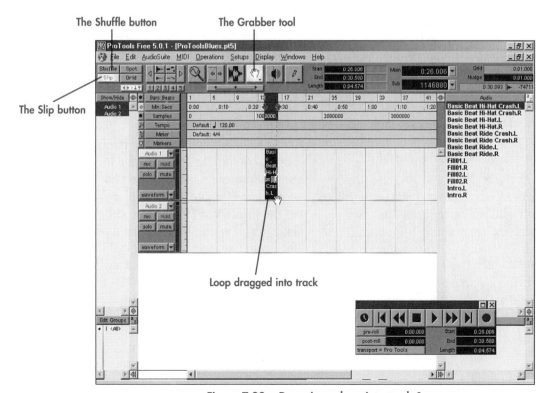

Figure 7.23   Dragging a loop into track 1.

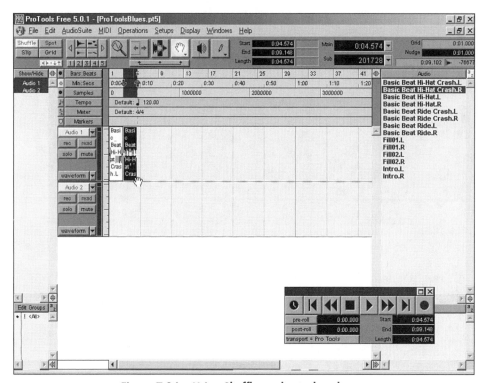

Figure 7.24   Using Shuffle mode to place loops.

Okay, now we need to get serious about this drum track stuff. First, though, you need to remove the loops you placed in the track. Click a loop in the track to highlight it, and then press Delete on your keyboard. The loop vanishes from the track, but it's still available in the Audio Regions List. Delete the second loop from the track in the same way. Now you're back to a clean slate.

Before we get started, notice that the loops you started off with have been converted to two loops each. For example, Pro Tools changed the Fill01.wav loop to two files, Fill01.L and Fill02.R. The L and the R mean left and right. You see, the original drum loops are stereo, but Pro Tools Free can handle only monophonic files. Pro Tools converted each

stereo file into two mono files, one for the left channel and one for the right. To re-create the stereo drums, you need to place the left version of the loop in the first track and the right version of the loop in the second track, as shown in Figure 7.25.

So to build the final drum tracks, all you have to do is drag copies of the loops into the tracks. You can use each loop as often as you want. For example, you can place four copies of the Basic Beat Hi-Hat.L and Basic Beat Hi-Hat.R in a row to create a drum pattern that's four times as long as the original loop. Just remember that every loop has an L and R version, and that those two versions must be exactly matched in the two tracks.

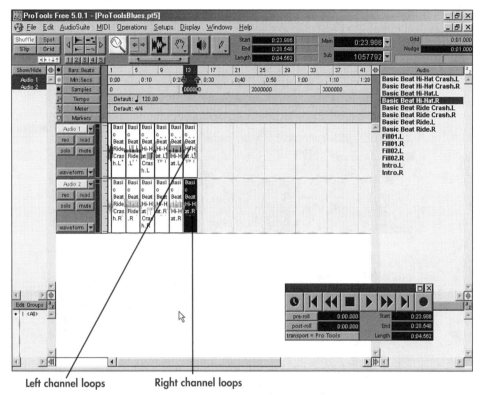

Left channel loops   Right channel loops

Figure 7.25   Re-creating the stereo drums.

Let's see how one might start building the drum track for a song. Make sure the Shuffle edit mode is active, and then perform these steps:

1. Drag Basic Beat Ride Crash.L into track 1, and Basic Beat Ride Crash.R into track 2.

2. Drag three copies of Basic Beat Ride.L into track 1, and three copies of Basic Beat Ride.R into track 2.

To better see what you've done, click the button that looks like a magnifying glass (Figure 7.26). This is the Zoomer tool. After selecting the Zoomer tool, click in the tracks. Pro Tools zooms in closer to the tracks, giving you a better view of the loop names, as shown in Figure 7.26.

Click the Play button in the Transport window to play your drum tracks. Notice something a little weird? The drum tracks are still not in stereo. This is because both channels are *panned center,* which just means that Pro Tools is playing both channels at equal volume through both the left and right outputs. This makes the drums sound as if they're all in the center of the stereo spectrum.

This problem is easy to fix. Go to the Windows menu, and select the Show Mix command. The Mix window, shown in Figure 7.27, springs into view. Anyone who's worked with sound systems or recording equipment will recognize this screen as a mixer.

The Zoomer tool

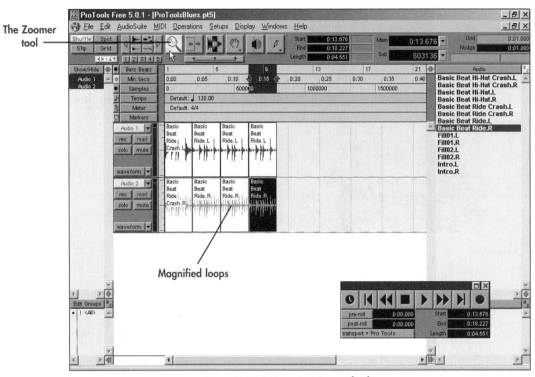

Magnified loops

Figure 7.26   Zooming in on the loops.

Track 1's pan slider

Track 2's pan slider

Channel strips

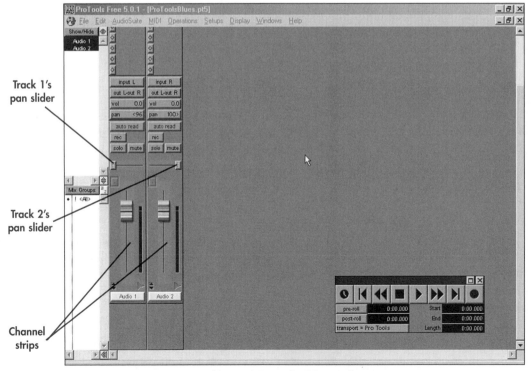

Figure 7.27   The Mix window.

Right now, the mixer shows two tracks, which are the same two tracks you've been working on in the Edit window. Each track has its own mixer channel strip, with which you can manipulate the associated track. (Depending on your screen resolution, you might have to scroll the Mix window down to get the view shown in the figure.)

To get the drums back into stereo, drag track 1's pan slider all the way to the left, and track 2's pan slider all the way to the right, as shown in the figure. Now, all of track 1's sound will come from the left and all of track 2's sound will come from the right. (This assumes, of course, that you're listening with some sort of stereo device, such as your trusty headphones or the monitoring system you set up back in Chapter 4.) Go ahead and listen. Stereo drums!

One last bit of organizing to make the Mix window easier to work with: naming the channel strips. See the white button at the bottom of each channel strip? The first is labeled Audio 1, and the second is labeled Audio 2. You can change these labels to something more meaningful, like … oh … Dog Breath and Yellow Shark (apologies to F.Z.). Or maybe Drums L and Drums R would work better, eh?

Double-click the Audio 1 button. The Audio 1 dialog box appears, as shown in Figure 7.28. In the Name the Track box, type **Drums L.** Then, click the Next button to move to the next channel strip, and type **Drums R** into the Name the Track box. Click OK, and view your new track names with suitable delight and awe. Figure 7.29 shows the newly named channel strips.

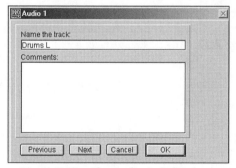

Figure 7.28   The Audio 1 dialog box.

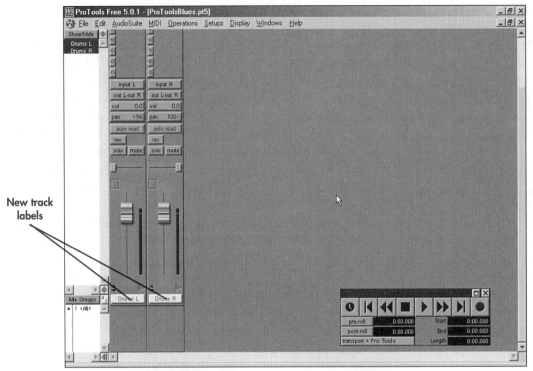

New track
labels

Figure 7.29   The session with renamed channel strips.

This could be the part of the chapter where I make you use the loops to create drum tracks for an entire song. Luckily for you, it's not that part at all. Still, feel free to experiment with the loops. When you're done, load the ProToolsBlues session from the Chapter07 folder of this book's disc. This sample session contains the complete drum track for the song "Pro Tools Blues." We'll do more with this session throughout the book.

The Least You Need to Know

◆ The first tracks you record should probably include drums or some sort of click track.

◆ Drums are usually recorded in stereo, which requires two tracks. Live drums, moreover, are usually recorded with five or more microphones, each microphone going to its own track.

◆ One alternative to live drums is drum loops, which are professionally recorded drum parts that you can string together to construct a drum track.

◆ Another alternative to live drums is a drum machine, although the resultant drum tracks may sound overly mechanical.

◆ Imported audio files appear in the Audio Regions List, from which you can drag them to tracks.

◆ A channel strip's pan slider enables you to position the track anywhere within the stereo spectrum.

In This Chapter

◆ Exploring studio effects

◆ Getting effects devices to serve double duty

◆ Using limiting and compression when recording

◆ Knowing when it's okay to record with effects

Chapter 8

Effects Used During Recording

Most home-studio budgets don't include money for tons of effects. In fact, a typical home studio is lucky to have a couple different effects that can be used simultaneously. For this reason, the budget-studio owners must come up with ways to get the most from their limited hardware. In a pro studio, most effects are added when the song is mixed, long after it's recorded. But in the home studio, effects must often be used both when recording and mixing. In this chapter, you learn why.

Effects?

Just exactly what am I referring to when I talk about effects? Lots of stuff, actually, especially because I'm using the term in a general way. (Another term I could use is *signal processors*.) By effects, I mean anything that manipulates or adds to a sound. Here's a list of the most common effects used in a recording studio:

◆ Reverb

◆ Echo

◆ Delay

◆ Compression

◆ Limiting

◆ EQ

◆ Flanging

◆ Phase shifting

◆ Chorus

Reverb

The effect with which most people are familiar is *reverberation*, usually shortened to "reverb." Reverb mimics the echoey interior of a large room. For example, stand in an empty gymnasium and yell something. That echolike sound you hear is your voice bouncing off the walls again and again, hundreds of times in a matter of a second or less.

Virtually every room reverberates, but the more stuff in the room (especially soft stuff like curtains and couches), the more reverb gets absorbed before it reaches your ears. Because recorded instruments—especially vocals—tend to sound very dry and unrealistic when played back, sound engineers use reverb effects to give these tracks a "roomy" sound, as if the track were recorded live rather than from right in front of a microphone.

A reverb effects unit—whether it comes in the form of a hardware box (Figure 8.1) or a software program (Figure 8.2)—enables the engineer to fine-tune the simulated reverberation in many ways. She can, for example, make a vocal sound like it was recorded in a bathtub. Then with a twist of a knob, she can change the bathtub to a gigantic theater. Reverb units have many other controls, too, that enable the engineer to get exactly the sound she wants.

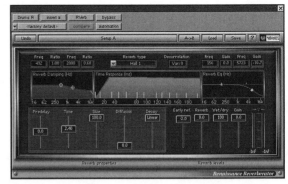

Figure 8.2   A software reverb effects unit.

Echo and Delay

Echo and delay are closely related to reverb. In fact, echo and delay are nothing more than reverb on a different timetable. As I said previously, reverb is hundreds of sound reflections a second. When you increase the time between each sound reflection, the result gets more and more "echoey" until you hear distinct repetitions of the original sound. When you stand in the mountains and yell "hello," you hear "hello, hello, hello …" This is echo.

Delay is nothing more than a single-repeat echo. Usually studio engineers use delay to "double" a sound. For example, if you play back a guitar track panned to the left and play back a slightly delayed (30 milliseconds or so) version of the guitar track on the right, it'll sound like two guitars playing the exact same thing. Delay can double instruments or make them sound really big. (Just as a side note, I should mention that the terms echo and delay are sometimes used interchangeably, but I'll stick to the more refined definitions I just explained.)

Figure 8.1   A hardware reverb effects unit.

Just as with any effects unit, echo and delay come in hardware and software form. Figure 8.3 shows a hardware effects unit that features not only echo and delay, but also many other effects such as reverb, chorus, and flanging. These fancy boxes have gotten really cheap, costing only around $200. Figure 8.4 shows the software version of a delay effect. In fact, it won't be long before you use this software effect in your Pro Tools projects.

Figure 8.3   A hardware multi-effects unit.

Figure 8.4   A software delay effects unit.

Compression and Limiting

Compression and limiting are as closely related as reverb and echo. Limiting is the easier of the two to understand. Think about how the ads on TV always seem louder than the shows. Annoying, yes? You could fix this problem with a limiter, which automatically turns down the volume of a sound when it gets too loud. Specifically, a limiter allows the level of a sound to get to a maximum point, after which the sound cannot get any louder.

A compressor is a limiter with a more liberal attitude. Just like a limiter, a compressor automatically reduces the level of sound when it gets too loud. Unlike a limiter, however, a compressor doesn't have an absolute limit on the level. Instead, a compressor reduces the level of overly loud sounds by a percentage. This enables a studio engineer to retain some of the dynamics of the original sound, which means that the performance can still get softer and louder, just not as much. Because compression and limiting manipulate the dynamic range of a sound, they are called *dynamic effects.*

Figure 8.5 shows a handy little compressor that you might see in a home studio, whereas Figure 8.6 shows the software compressor that comes with Pro Tools Free. Note that most compressors can also act as limiters, because both effects are really the same thing, just set to different values.

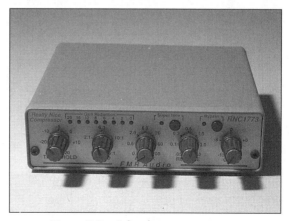

Figure 8.5   A hardware compressor.

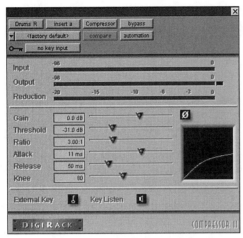

Figure 8.6   A software compressor.

EQ

EQ is short for *equalization.* What's being
equalized? The various frequencies present in a
sound. Remember when we talked about speakers and microphones? We said that they should
have a flat frequency response. Well, suppose
you have a microphone that, for some reason,
always boosts sound in the 2000Hz range. An
equalizer lets you take that single frequency
and turn it down again. In short, an equalizer
is a super-duper tone control.

There are two kinds of EQ: graphic and
parametric. Figure 8.7 shows a graphic EQ.
Notice how the many sliders that represent the
different frequencies create a picture of the
resultant frequency content. Graphic EQs give
a recording engineer immense power for shap-
ing a sound, because he or she can cut or boost
any number of frequencies up to the number
of available sliders.

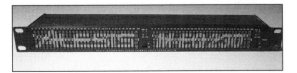

Figure 8.7   A hardware graphic EQ.

Figure 8.8 shows a parametric EQ, which,
due to its limited controls, is the type often built
in to mixers. With a parametric EQ, you can
usually manipulate only a few frequencies at a
time. How many depends on the EQ, with one,
two, or three being typical. Often, one control
(the *sweep* control) selects the frequency to
manipulate and another (the *gain* control) determines how much the EQ boosts or cuts the
chosen frequency. Sometimes an extra control
sets the *bandwidth* (the number of frequencies
surrounding the selected frequency) affected by
the changes. This extra control is called Q.

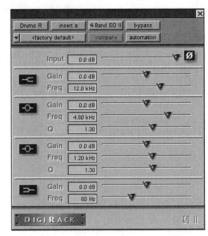

Figure 8.8   A parametric EQ.

Flanging, Phase Shifting, and Chorus

The effects of flanging, phase shifting, and
chorus might sound similar to the untrained ear,
but there are important differences. Flanging is
related to delay in that it's a time-based effect.
Instead of having a single delay time, however,
a flanger varies the length of time between
delayed copies of the original sound and combines them to create a constantly changing filter. I know, I know. That probably doesn't
describe the sound very well. You'll just have
to hear a flanger for yourself, but imagine a jet
taking off, and you'll have some idea.

A phase shifter sounds similar to a flanger, but is usually more subtle, thanks to the different way it produces its effect. How? Okay, you asked for it. A phase shifter constantly changes the phase relationship between the original sound and copies of the sound. Sorry, but you asked for it. Again, you really need to hear the effect for yourself. The closest I can come to describing phasing is the word "smoky." The famous reggae artist, Bob Marley, used a phase shifter when playing some of his rhythm guitar parts.

Chorus is also a similar effect, and does, in fact, work much like a flanger. The chorus effect, however, "detunes" the original sound and creates longer delays between copies of the sound, making the original sound big and sumptuous. The effect is called chorus because the result is like taking a single voice and duplicating it many times, such as when a dozen people sing in unison. Figure 8.9 shows a software flanging device. Andy Summers, the guitarist for the 1980's band The Police, used tons of chorus with his rhythm guitar parts, so much so that it's practically his trademark.

Because I know you're dying to hear some of these effects for yourself, I recorded a guitar part and applied different effects to the result. You can find the audio files in the Chapter08\Effects folder of this book's CD-ROM. The files are in standard .wav format, so you should be able to play them with any of your computer audio players. Here's a list of files and their descriptions:

- **Dry.wav.** This is the dry guitar recording. That is, it contains no effects.
- **SmallRoom.wav.** This recording uses reverb to simulate the sound of a small room.
- **MediumRoom.wav.** This recording uses reverb to simulate the sound of a medium-size room.

- **LargeRoom.wav.** This recording uses reverb to simulate the sound of a large room.
- **SlapBack.wav.** The slapback effect is generated by a delay that generates a single copy of the sound delayed around 70ms.
- **DelayDoubled.wav.** This is a stereo recording that uses delay to make one guitar sound like two, one on each side. The delay time is about 35ms.
- **DelayGhost.wav.** This sample uses a single delay to "ghost" the guitar. Specifically, it's a delay of about one second, with the single repeat much quieter than the main guitar track.
- **Echo.wav.** This version of the guitar track uses a delay with "feedback" to produce the sound that most people think of as echo.
- **DelayEcho.wav.** This is another echo effect where the repeats are more subtle.
- **Flanger.wav.** This is the guitar with flanging.
- **UltraFastFlanger.wav.** This is what you get when you crank a flanger's speed way up. Underwater guitar!
- **Chorus.wav.** This is the guitar recorded with chorus. Compare this to flanging. On the picked chords near the end of the track, you can really hear how the chorus "detunes" the guitar images to create the effect. In fact, this chorus is set too high for most uses.

Figure 8.9   A software-based flanger.

Effect Recording

What you've just read is little more than an introduction to the world of effects. You'll learn a lot more about these effects when you get to Part 3 of this book, which covers mixing. Right now, you only need to know what the various effects are and generally what they do. If we weren't talking about home recording on a low budget, I probably wouldn't even have mentioned these effects yet—well, maybe limiting and compression, which are actually important recording tools.

As I said before, home studios rarely have dozens of different effects units at their beck and call. This lack of hardware can lead to trouble. For example, suppose you have only two compressors, but have four instruments that need to be compressed? The way to solve this problem is to compress two of the instruments as they're being recorded and the other two when you're doing the mix.

Just Push Play

You folks with computers may be smirking right now, thinking, "My effects are software based, and I can use as many simultaneous copies as I want." Theoretically, that's true and is one of the big advantages of a computer-based studio. Software can be duplicated again and again in memory at no cost, whereas every hardware device you add costs big bucks.

No computer, however, can run unlimited software simultaneously. The more effects you use, the more processor power you need. You'll quickly discover that you can't have as many effects as you thought. Again, the way around this limitation is to use some effects during recording and others during mix-down.

Confused? Suppose, for example, that you need to record a drummer, bassist, and singer together. You have two compressors, but you need to use them on the kick drum, the snare drum, the bass, and the vocals. You could run out and buy two more compressors, but if your wallet looks anything like mine, that's out of the question. Instead, you do this:

1. Plug the snare-drum mic into compressor 1, which then connects to channel 1 on the recorder.

2. Plug the kick-drum mic into compressor 2, which then connects to channel 2 on the recorder.

3. Plug the bass microphone into channel 3 of the recorder.

4. Plug the vocal mic into channel 4 of the recorder.

5. Make your recording.

Now you have a four-track recording with the first two tracks compressed. (We'll overlook the fact that a snare drum and kick drum are far from a full drum set! Just assume that two overhead mics were also recorded.) The second two tracks—the bass and the vocals—still need to be compressed. Luckily, because you used the compressors on the first two tracks when recording, the compressors are now free to be used on the second two tracks during mixing. Two compressors doing the work of four.

Now for the downside: When you use effects during recording, you're stuck with the results. If you don't like the result, the only solution is to record the tracks over. This isn't true during the mixing process, because, as you'll see when you get to Part 3 of the book, it's easy during the mix to tweak effects until they're just right.

Recommended Recorded Effects

Although dealing with a limited number of effect devices is one reason to record tracks with effects, it's not the only one. In fact, recording engineers frequently use one class of effects—dynamic effects—when recording. Musicians, too, have their own effects units that they probably want to use when recording.

Recording with Limiting

Remember when we talked about keeping the level of your tracks from peaking into the red? Some instruments, due to their dynamic nature, are infamously hard to record without distortion. Drums, again, are the worst culprit, with the human voice coming in second.

The usual scenario goes like this: You get the drums all mic'ed up and then ask the drummer to play so you can set the recording levels. Once you're satisfied with the levels, you make a first attempt to record the band. But now the drummer gets into the song. He or she starts drumming a lot harder, and all your drum channels leap into the red. Arrrrggghhhhh! One take thrown away.

To avoid this problem, put a limiter on each drum mic and set the limiter so that the drum tracks can never exceed a safe level. You still should try to get the track levels right in the first place, so that the limiters never have anything to do. But it's good to know that, if you're caught by surprise, the limiter will prevent the track from being ruined.

Just Push Play

Remember that too much limiting or compression squishes the life out of a track, so try to compromise between the actual track level and when the limiter springs into action. Don't just crank everything up too high and force the limiter to do the work.

Recording with Compression

Many recording engineers also routinely compress drum tracks or vocals during recording. In this case, the effect is not just a safety mechanism, but also one that's meant to smooth out an overly dynamic sound so that it stays at an even keel throughout the song. This use of compression can also be applied during mixing.

How about a real-world example? I once recorded an opera singer in my home studio. In a single piece, he would go from quiet passages into powerful lines that drove the track level straight into the red. In cases like these, just turning down the level of the track isn't a good solution, because, in order to allow room for the louder passages, the quieter passages end up recorded too low. In the case of my opera singer, during the quiet passages, the vocal got lost in the music, whereas the loud passage drowned out the music.

Imagine if music was like water. You take a big box and pour the music in. Because music tends to be very dynamic by nature, your water-music is always sloshing around in the box, creating little waves and peaks, as shown in Figure 8.10.

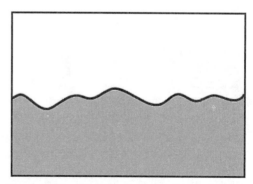

Figure 8.10   **Music is not unlike water sloshing around in a box.**

Now imagine that a singer's voice is like a rope flicking around above your water-music box. As the rope moves around, sometimes it's in the water, and sometimes it's above the water. When the rope-voice is in the water, it's being drowned out. The deeper in the music, the harder the voice is to hear. The higher the rope is above the water, the louder the voice is, as shown in Figure 8.11.

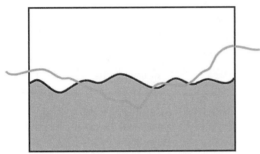

Figure 8.11   A rope-voice whipping around above the water-music box.

The idea is to straighten the rope a little, so that it stays mostly above the water, but not too high above the water or too deep into the water, as shown in Figure 8.12. The force that straightens out the rope is the compressor we were talking about.

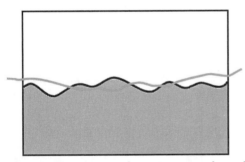

Figure 8.12   A straighter rope-voice above the water-music box.

So getting back to my opera singer, by placing a compressor on the vocal mic, I squeezed down the loud parts so they were closer in volume to the quieter parts. This not only helped keep the track out of the red, but also allowed the vocal to be heard over the music throughout the entire song.

Notes from the Track Sheet

The trick with vocal compression is to be sure that the vocal varies in level enough that it's still representative of the singer's dynamic performance. You want to tame the vocal, not squish it flat.

Recording with Other Effects

Musicians often bring their own effects into the studio. Guitarists, especially, like to record with their effects on, just as they do when performing live. Because the guitarist's basic sound includes the effects, you'll want to record the sound intact.

A perfect example is a distorted guitar. Asking a heavy-metal guitarist not to use his distortion is ridiculous. Not only does this make the guitarist want to use your eyes as ashtrays, it doesn't even make sense. You want to record the sound of the instrument, and, in this case, the instrument is a distorted guitar. The same is true to a lesser degree for effects like phase shifting, flanging, and chorus—as long as these effects are used by the player during a live performance.

Reverb, on the other hand, is rarely recorded onto a track, usually added only during the mixing process. But even reverb has exceptions. If a guitarist uses the reverb on his or her amp as a basic part of his or her overall sound, he or she'd have a compelling argument for demanding that you record his or her guitar sound intact, reverb and all.

Often, the effects a player uses when recording come in the form of "stomp boxes," those little electronic dingies that the musician turns on and off with a foot switch. These would be the same effects he or she uses when performing live. Figure 8.13, for example, shows a distortion stomp box for heavy-metal guitar. You could also use your own studio devices to add flanging, phase shifting, and other effects during recording. Just remember, *once you record with effects, the effects can never be removed from the track.*

Figure 8.13   A distortion stomp box.

You've now had a brief introduction to effects and how you might use them when recording tracks. As I said before, you'll learn a lot more about studio effects later in this book.

The Least You Need to Know

◆ Effects manipulate or add to a sound.

◆ Reverb mimics the echoey interior of a room.

◆ Delay is essentially a single-repeat echo, often used to double record sounds.

◆ A limiter allows the level of a sound to get to a maximum point, after which the sound cannot get any louder, whereas a compressor reduces the level of overly loud sound by a percentage, enabling the sound to retain some of its dynamic character.

◆ An equalizer changes the level of specific frequencies of sound.

◆ Flangers, phase shifters, and choruses sound somewhat similar but produce their effects in different ways.

In This Chapter

- ◆ Understanding the overdubbing process
- ◆ Exploring the steps required for overdubbing
- ◆ Overdubbing on all-in-one digital workstations
- ◆ Overdubbing with Pro Tools Free

Overdubbing

In the old days, entire bands were recorded at one time, but most studio sessions these days involve laying down a couple of basic tracks and then adding instruments and vocals one at a time. This is especially true of today's multi-instrumentalist, singer/songwriters who often record all the parts of a song themselves. After all, even the most talented musician has only two hands, even if listening to their recording makes you think otherwise. In this chapter, you learn the secrets of overdubbing, the process by which you can add tracks to your existing sessions.

The Overdubbing Process

Conceptually, overdubbing is a simple process. It simply means recording new parts for a song while listening to the existing parts. A couple of chapters back, for example, you learned to use drum loops to create a drum track for a song named "Pro Tools Blues." Obviously, this drum track alone isn't much of a song—in fact, it isn't even much of a drum solo! To complete the recording, guitar, bass, and vocals must be added to the drums.

How you go about adding new tracks to your projects depends on how you recorded your basic tracks in the first place. If you recorded an entire band, you may only need to overdub some vocals. On the other hand, if you recorded only drums, you still have a lot of work in front of you. Let's start with vocals, shall we?

Dealing with Vocals

In most cases, vocals are the most important element of the songs you record, because people most identify with and recognize vocals. Ask someone to sing the first verse of "Dream On" by Aerosmith, and he'll probably at least be able to hum a melody, but ask him or her to sing the same song's bass line, and you'll get a baffled look. Heck, most nonmusicians don't even know what a bass line *is*.

Because vocals are so important to popular music, they almost always get special handling. Specifically, it would be very rare for a song's final vocal tracks not to be overdubbed sometime after the band has recorded the rest of the song. Typically, the band records the song (or the song's basic tracks, whatever they decide those tracks will be) along with a *scratch vocal*. To create a scratch vocal, the vocalist sings along with the band, just as he or she would in a live situation, with the vocal going to a separate track on the recorder. However, this vocal track is used only as a guide, so the whole group knows where they are in the song.

When the group has recorded all of the instrumental tracks, they throw away the scratch vocal (unless it happened to come out really great), and the singer overdubs the final vocals, taking his or her time to get everything just right. The rest of the band may or may not even choose to hang around the studio. After all, their parts are complete. Even when you're a solo artist who plans to construct the song track by track, the final vocals almost always come last—although, again, a scratch vocal keeps you informed of where you are in the song.

Overdubbing with a Band

To clarify the overdubbing process, here's a typical scenario. The four-piece group Willy Walnuts wants to record a song's basic rhythm

tracks all at once, in order to retain as much of the instrumental interplay and live feel as possible. However, they will add other tracks, especially vocals, later:

1. The drummer, bassist, and guitarist record the basic rhythm tracks, with the singer recording a scratch vocal.
2. Listening to the recording created in Step 1, the guitarist overdubs a second rhythm guitar to complement the previously recorded rhythm guitar.

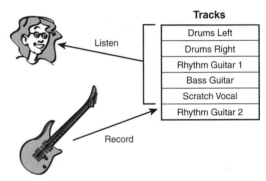

Figure 9.1   Recording a second rhythm track.

3. Listening to the recording created in Steps 1 and 2, the guitarist overdubs a guitar solo for the song's bridge.

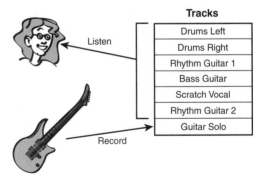

Figure 9.2   Overdubbing a guitar solo.

4. Listening to the recording created in Steps 1 through 3, the vocalist replaces the scratch lead vocal with a more carefully recorded final track.

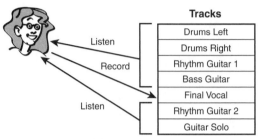

Figure 9.3   Overdubbing the final vocal.

5. Listening to the recording created in Steps 1 through 4, the background vocalists add their harmony parts to the new final lead vocal.

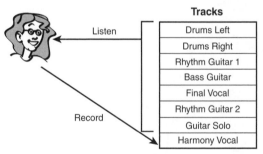

Figure 9.4   Overdubbing the harmony vocal.

Overdubbing for a Solo Artist

For the one-person-band scenario, the steps are a little more tedious, but still similar.

1. The artist records the song's drum tracks, which also act as the song's click track.

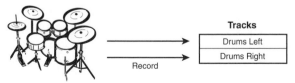

Figure 9.5   Recording the drum or click track.

2. Listening to the recording created in Step 1, the artist records the main rhythm instrument, typically guitar or some sort of keyboard.

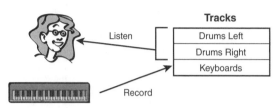

Figure 9.6   Overdubbing a rhythm instrument.

3. Listening to the recording created in Steps 1 and 2, the artist records a scratch vocal as a guide for recording the remaining tracks.

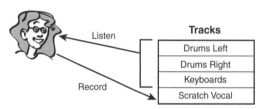

Figure 9.7   Overdubbing a scratch vocal.

4. Listening to the recording created in Steps 1 through 3, the artist records a second rhythm instrument.

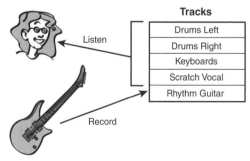

Figure 9.8   Overdubbing another rhythm instrument.

5. Listening to the recording created in Steps 1 through 4, the artist records the song's bass line.

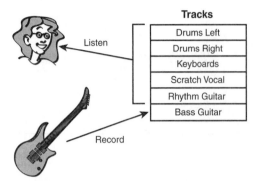

Figure 9.9   Recording the bass track.

6. Listening to the recording created in Steps 1 through 5, the artist records any instrumental solos.

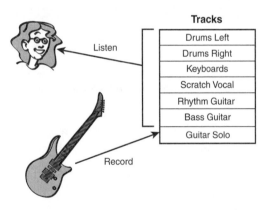

Figure 9.10   Recording a solo.

7. Listening to the recording created in Steps 1 through 6, the artist replaces the scratch vocal track with the final vocal track.

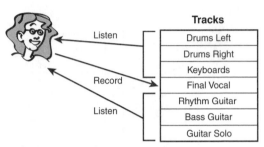

Figure 9.11   Overdubbing the final lead vocal.

8. Listening to the recording created in Steps 1 through 7, the artist records any background vocals.

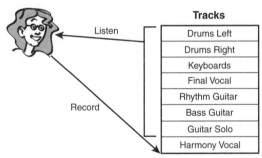

Figure 9.12   Overdubbing a background vocal.

This list can be customized to taste and need. You might, for example, prefer to record your bass line before you record additional rhythm instruments, or you might decide to finalize your vocals before laying down instrumental solo tracks.

Steps 1 through 3, though, are carved in stone—sort of. In the case of Step 1, you have to start with some sort of click track to control the song's tempo. If you're using drums, the drums might as well be your click track, too, eh?

Vocal tracks and solos make sense musically only with the appropriate accompaniment. (In most cases, what makes a song identifiable is a melody over chord progression.) For that reason, you'll almost always want to record a guitar or keyboard rhythm track before any melodies.

Step 3 is sort of optional. If you know the song well, and can record all parts without following the lyrics, you can get away without a scratch vocal. In most cases, though, the scratch vocal makes the overdubbing task easier.

Notes from the Track Sheet

Notice something similar about every step of each scenario? You always listen to previously recorded tracks as you record a new one. This, in a nutshell, is the process of overdubbing.

Getting the Job Done, in General

The overdubbing process is easy to define, but accomplishing it requires knowledge of your recording equipment. Virtually every recording setup can handle overdubbing, but the details of how it works vary from system to system. In general, though, you set previously recorded tracks to playback, arm for recording the track on which you'll overdub a new part, and then record.

Suppose you have a three-piece band that has recorded the following basic tracks:

Track 1: Drums left

Track 2: Drums right

Track 3: Bass guitar

Track 4: Rhythm guitar

Now, you want to overdub a two-part vocal. You might do this:

1. Set tracks 1 through 4 for playback.
2. Plug a microphone into track 5 and arm the track for recording.
3. Record the first vocal part onto track 5 (while listening to tracks 1 through 4, of course).
4. Set track 5 for playback.
5. Route the microphone to track 6 and arm the track for recording.
6. Record the second vocal part onto track 6 (while listening to tracks 1 through 5).

That's the general procedure, but how does it work in the real world?

Getting the Job Done with an All-in-One Workstation

Digital workstations are all different, so it's impossible to tell you exactly how to use them all. That's why they give you manuals, dude! No matter the hardware, though, for overdubbing you still need to know two general tasks: how to route microphone inputs to different channels, and how to set channels for record or play.

When routing microphones to appropriate tracks, you can usually just plug a mic into the mixer's first mic input and then reroute that input to different tracks as needed. That is, the mic input that's associated with channel 1 on the mixer doesn't necessarily need to be routed to channel 1. It can go to whatever channel you want. This convenience saves you from having to constantly plug and unplug the microphone.

With the Tascam 788 Digital Portastudio, associating an input with a channel requires nothing more than pressing two buttons.

Specifically, you hold down the Input button for the input and then press the Select button for the channel to which you want to route the input, as shown in Figure 9.13.

To assign input 2 ...

... then press ...

Figure 9.13   Routing an input to a channel.

To arm a track for recording on the Tascam 788, you need only press the Rec Ready button right above the channel's fader (level control), as shown in Figure 9.14. When you do, the channel's red record light starts blinking. When you start recording, by pressing the Record and Play buttons on the transport controls, the record light for each armed channel stops blinking and glows steady red. Taking a track out of record mode puts it into playback mode.

Record button for track 3   Record and Play buttons

Figure 9.14   Arming a track for record.

Getting the Job Done with Pro Tools

Just as when using an all-in-one workstation, to overdub with Pro Tools you need to know how to route inputs to tracks and how to switch between play and record mode. A little mouse-clicking is all it takes to get these jobs done, but the type of Pro Tools setup you have determines the choices you have.

If you're using Pro Tools Free with a standard computer sound card, you only have one mic input and that input is automatically routed to all eight tracks. In other words, all you have to do is place a track into record mode to receive input from the computer's sound card.

Depending on your sound card, though, you have different types of inputs. At the very least, you have a mic input and a line input. Whichever of these inputs is selected for your computer is the one that Pro Tools receives. To change the sound card input, you need to bring up the sound card's mixer.

Let's see how this works by adding a track to the "Pro Tools Blues" session. Start up Pro Tools and follow these steps:

1. Select the Open Session command from the File menu.
2. In the dialog box, find the Pro Tools Blues session and select it. Click the Open button to load it.
3. From the File menu, select the New Track command.

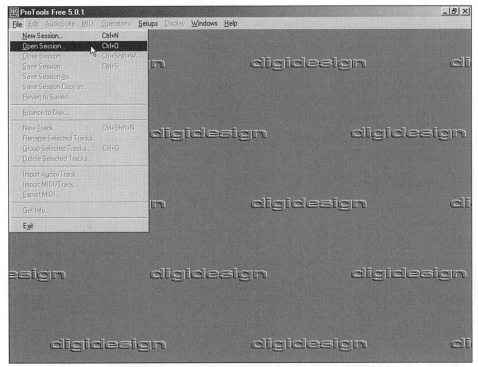

Figure 9.15   Selecting the Open Session command.

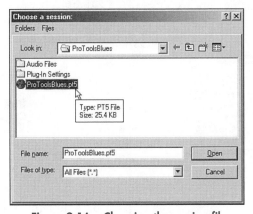

Figure 9.16   Choosing the session file.

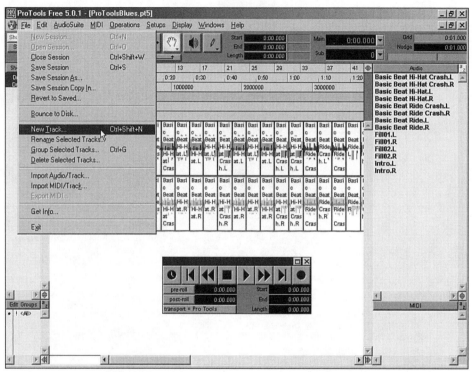

Figure 9.17   Selecting the New Track command.

4. When the New Track dialog appears, create six new audio tracks.

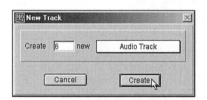

Figure 9.18   Creating six audio tracks.

5. Select the New Track command again, and this time create one stereo master fader track.

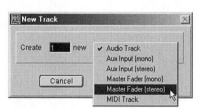

Figure 9.19   Adding the Master Fader track.

6. Select the Show Mix command from the Windows menu.

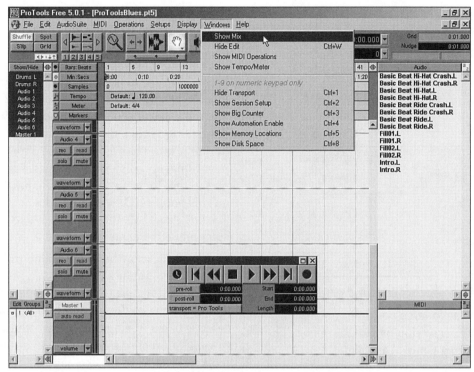

Figure 9.20   Selecting the Show Mix command.

At this point, you have eight audio tracks—which is the most you can use with Pro Tools Free. You also have a master fader track, which acts as a global volume control for the entire session. In other words, when you change the level of the master fader, you change the level of the mixed output of all the tracks.

Now you need to get set up to record your next track. If you're going to pop a microphone in front of a guitar amp (or some other instrument's amp), you need to use your sound card's microphone input. In my case, I chose to use my POD amp simulator and plugged it into the sound card's line input. In either case, you have to tell your computer which input to use. Here's how with Windows Me:

1. From the Start menu, bring up the Control Panel, and double-click the Sounds and Multimedia icon.

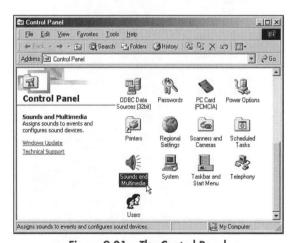

Figure 9.21   The Control Panel.

2. When the Sounds and Multimedia Properties dialog box appears, select the Audio tab.

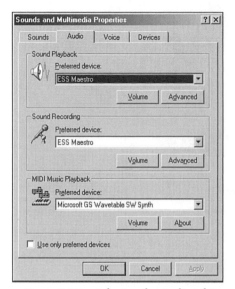

Figure 9.22 **Selecting the Audio tab.**

3. Click the Volume button in the Sound Recording section of the dialog box. The Recording Control appears.

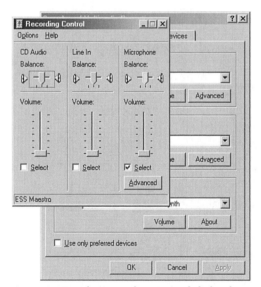

Figure 9.23 **The Recording Control dialog box.**

4. Put a check mark in the Select box for the input you want to use.

The input you've chosen to use will now be routed to Pro Tools Free. The Volume slider in the Recording Control determines the level of the input being sent to Pro Tools. Now all you have to do is click the third track's Rec button to put it into record mode, start Pro Tools recording, and play your new part while listening to the drum track. In the Chapter09 folder of this book's CD, you can find a new version of the "Pro Tools Blues" project, which has an overdubbed rhythm guitar part.

Now you know how to overdub tracks in a session. You might have run into a problem with something called *latency*, though. Latency is when what you're playing into Pro Tools sounds like it's being delayed, which can make it tough to record a decent track. In the next chapter, you learn how to handle latency as you add even more tracks to your song.

The Least You Need to Know

◆ Overdubbing is recording new parts for a song while listening to the existing parts.

◆ Because vocals are so important to popular music, they almost always get special handling.

◆ A *scratch vocal* is used as a guide, so that the whole group knows where they are in the song.

◆ Vocal tracks and solos make sense musically only with the appropriate accompaniment, so you'll almost always want to record a guitar or keyboard rhythm track before any melodies.

◆ In general, when overdubbing, you set previously recorded tracks to playback, arm for recording the track on which you'll overdub a new part, and then record.

◆ For overdubbing you need to know how to route microphone inputs to different channels and how to set channels for record or play.

In This Chapter

◆ Punching-in to fix mistakes

◆ Using virtual tracks

◆ Enhancing performances with doubling

◆ Minimizing the effects of latency

10

Improving a Performance

Once you've recorded your tracks, you still may not be done recording. In these days when consumers expect studio recordings to be virtually perfect, studio engineers spend a lot of time tweaking recorded tracks. Some techniques used to get a recording close to perfection include punching-in, doubling, and choosing between multiple performances. In this chapter, you learn to apply these important techniques to your own recording projects.

The Tricks of the Trade

A professional recording studio draws upon many tricks and techniques to improve the recordings created by its clients. Luckily, you can use many of these tricks in your own studio—even if your studio is just a computer running Pro Tools Free. With a little knowledge and skill, you can fine-tune your tracks to near perfection—or at least as perfect as your skills as a musician and recordist permit. The most common tricks used to improve recorded performances include the following:

◆ Punching-in
◆ Virtual tracks
◆ Doubling and tripling

These techniques are only the tip of the iceberg, with plenty more that you can employ not only as you record, but also as you mix your tracks down to a stereo master. Most recorded performances, however, can benefit from the application of one or more of these basic techniques.

Punching-In

Ask any musician who has been in a recording studio, and he or she will tell you that no matter how well you know your part, when the recording starts, the pressure to create a great track makes it hard to perform. In a live performance, every mistake is history the instant it happens. On the other hand, in a studio, your mistakes are recorded and can be played back again and again. These mistakes can't be allowed to make it to the final mix. Add the knowledge that recording time costs big bucks, and you can see how the recording musician might get a little nervous when the record light turns red.

Strangely, this desire to "get it right the first time" boils over into the home studio, where you usually have all the time you need to get it right. Capturing a perfect performance, even after many takes, is often an allusive goal. We're musicians, after all, not machines. The good news is that you don't have to turn in a perfect performance. If you manage to record a good one, you can make it great by using a few studio tricks. One of the most common is *punching-in*, which means rerecording a small part of a performance. Here's how it usually goes:

1. The musician records a track, which is a good take except for a small mistake.

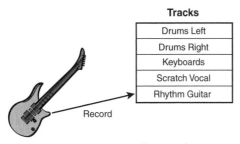

Figure 10.1   Recording a take.

2. The recording engineer listens to the flawed track, making a note of when the mistake begins and ends.

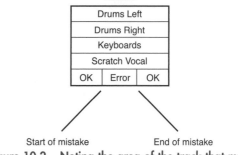

Figure 10.2   Noting the area of the track that must be fixed.

3. While listening to the playback, the musician replays the performance.

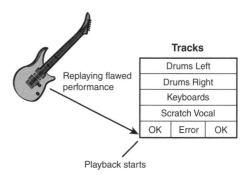

Figure 10.3   Repeating the performance.

4. When the song reaches the mistake, the engineer "punches" the record button, replacing the mistake with the musician's current performance.

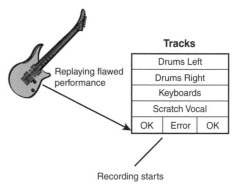

Figure 10.4   Recording over the mistake.

5. At the end of the mistake, the engineer punches the record button again, taking the machine out of record.

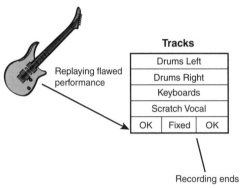

Figure 10.5   Ending the punch-in.

Correcting errors this way, enables you to keep the good parts of a performance, while replacing the bad parts. The musician is more relaxed, because he or she knows that he or she has recorded almost all of the performance well and

only needs to fix the flawed area. If he or she makes other mistakes during the playback of the good areas of the track, it doesn't matter, because recording takes place only over the flawed part of the performance. When done correctly, punching-in can leave you with a seamless, perfect track.

To make the process even easier, many recording systems provide automatic punching-in and punching-out. You tell the recorder when to start recording and when to stop, and the recorder takes care of the rest. You just start the machine, and then sit back while the musician fixes his or her mistake.

With Pro Tools Free, punching-in is a snap. Just arm the track you want to record, and then drag the mouse cursor in the area above the tracks to highlight the area to rerecord, as shown in Figure 10.6. When you start recording, Pro Tools records only inside the selected area.

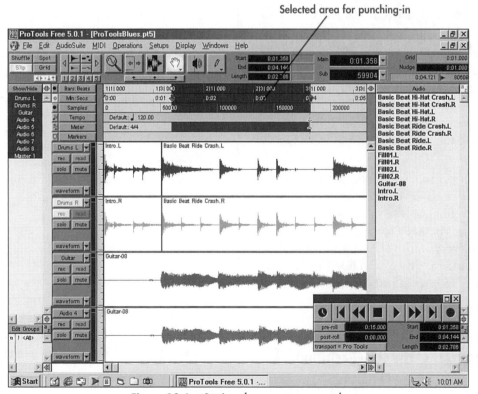

Figure 10.6   Setting the area to rerecord.

Multiple Performances and Virtual Tracks

Although I've used the word *perfect* a lot in the previous paragraphs, the truth is that there's really no such thing as a perfect performance. Often, one performance is just as technically perfect as another, even though both performances are significantly different. A good example might be an improvisational guitar solo.

When recording tracks in a studio, it's common practice to keep every performance, even when the musician in question thinks he or she can do better. One way to do this is to record, on separate tracks, different performances of the same part, giving the engineer the option of choosing the one that seems to work best for the song.

Another way to try different performances is with *virtual tracks*, a computerized version of the same technique. The advantage of virtual tracks is that you need to tie up only a single track in the project. (If you're a guitarist, another way to get a perfect track is to hire Eric Clapton, but most of us can't afford this solution. I've tried begging, but the restraining order has forced me to stay away from Eric.)

Multiple Tracks, the Old-Fashioned Way

Take our fictional group Willy Walnuts. Please. The guitarist, Felix, records a solo, and even

though everyone likes it, Felix thinks he can do better. Rather than recording over the first solo, the engineer—who knows that the first solo was pretty darn good and doesn't want to lose it—sets Felix up on another track, and the guitarist gives it another try. Now, the group has two different solos from which to choose. Felix could even try again on a third track.

After Felix decides that he's done the best he can (knowing guitarists, that would be about 35 solos later, would be my guess), the engineer, producer, and the group listen back to the song. The engineer mutes all of the guitar-solo tracks (Figure 10.7) except one, and everyone listens (except the guitarist, who, even though he's turned in lots of cool solos, still isn't happy and has left the studio in search of gummy worms and other comfort food).

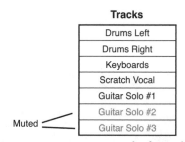

Figure 10.7   Listening to the first solo.

After listening to the first solo, the engineer mutes it, and unmutes the second (Figure 10.8), and everyone listens again. After listening to all the solos, they decide on the best one.

Tracks

| Drums Left |
| Drums Right |
| Keyboards |
| Scratch Vocal |
| Guitar Solo #1 |
| Guitar Solo #2 |
| Guitar Solo #3 |

Muted

Figure 10.8   Listening to the second solo.

Virtual Tracks, the New-Fangled Way

The technique of recording multiple performances is also the idea behind virtual tracks, except to use virtual tracks, you need to have some sort of computer-based recording system. Most recording software and all-in-one workstations can accommodate virtual tracks. With virtual tracks, you record many takes of a performance, but all the takes are associated with only a single track. To listen back to a take, you plug it into the track.

Let's again consider Willy Walnuts and their guitarist extraordinaire, Felix. We'll spin the group back in time and make Felix redo all his solos, only this time we'll use virtual tracks. (No need to worry about Felix's fragile self-esteem. Because we brought him back in time, he doesn't remember all the other solos he played and didn't like the first time.) Let's say Felix tries three versions of his solo. Figure 10.9 shows how the session might look.

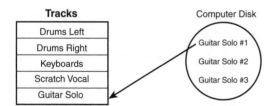

Figure 10.9   Three guitar solos as virtual tracks.

As you can see in the figure, only one track is assigned to the guitar solo, but all three solos are still stored on the computer's disk. Currently, as indicated by the arrow, the first solo is assigned to the track. After listening to the song with the first solo, the engineer assigns the second guitar solo to the track, as shown in Figure 10.10. Everyone listens to the song again. And so it goes: multiple performances that magically require only a single track.

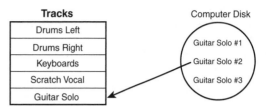

Figure 10.10   Assigning the second solo to the track.

Doubling, Tripling, Quadrupling ... Ad Infinitum

Most people would say that bigger is better, and in the recording studio, the same is true. Studio engineers go out of their way to make everything sound as big as possible. In the early days of recording, reverb was the tool that added the "coolness" factor to recordings, especially vocals. Today, however, reverb is often used modestly with other recording techniques being favored to make sounds not only bigger but more "in your face."

One of the most common techniques is the layering of multiple performances. For example, a guitarist might record the same part two or more times, so that all the parts can be mixed together in various ways to make the guitar part more sonically interesting or to seem as if it's coming from everywhere in the stereo spectrum.

Imagine a live, three-piece band comprised of drums, bass, and guitar. (Yep, it's Willy Walnuts.) Now add to the band a second guitarist who plays in unison with the first player. You end up with a richer guitar sound. You also end up with two guitarist who fight over who gets the solos, but that's another story. This richer sound is exactly the effect that they go for in a studio.

Notes from the Track Sheet

I've heard of the same part being layered 10 times or more, with each part being only slightly different in tone or timing. In fact, the story goes that there are more than 200 vocal tracks in the classic Queen opus "Bohemian Rhapsody." Can you imagine putting all that together?

Vocals are another type of track that are frequently layered. Just adding one extra take to a vocal can make the vocal sound incredibly rich and omnipresent. During the recording of a song, multiple vocal tracks are pretty much the rule, with the producer deciding what to do with all the extra tracks during the mix-down.

Just Push Play

Having doubled and tripled tracks of the same part gives the recording's mixing engineer a lot of power. Sometimes the extra tracks are all panned to the same location, which gives the performance a kind of chorus effect. Other times, they're panned to various places in the stereo spectrum, resulting in a huge, omnipresent sound. However they're used, doubled (or more) tracks always add an interesting sonic texture to a performance.

Easy Doubling with Pro Tools Free

In any studio, you can double tracks simply by playing and recording the same part a second time. When you're recording on a computer, however, there's a tricky way to get a doubled performance. You can simply make a copy of an existing track, and then slightly delay the copy. A small amount of delay makes the new track sound like a second instrument playing the same part as the first. To see how this works, first start up Pro Tools Free. Then, load last chapter's "Pro Tools Blues" project, and follow these steps:

1. Display the Edit window, and select the Guitar audio file in the Audio Regions list.

2. Drag the file name into the fourth track, so that the audio lines up with the version in the third track.

3. Select the Zoomer tool, and then click the Edit window three times to zoom in on the audio.

4. Select the Grabber tool, and drag the new guitar audio region slightly to the right, which delays it compared with the first version in the third track. (Be sure that you select the Slip button first.)

5. Switch to the Mix window. Pan the original guitar part to the left until the pan value reads <72, and pan the new guitar part to the right until the pan value reads 72>.

Now go ahead and play the new session. Notice how rich the rhythm guitar part sounds. To really hear the effect, listen with headphones.

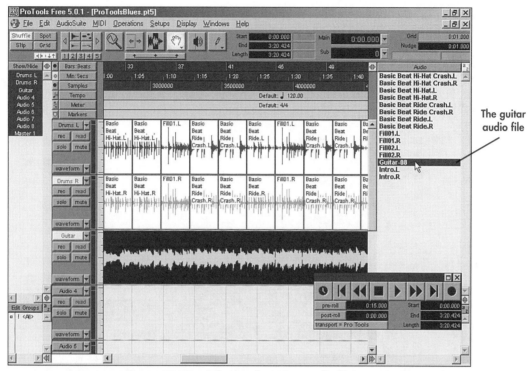

Figure 10.11   Selecting the guitar audio file.

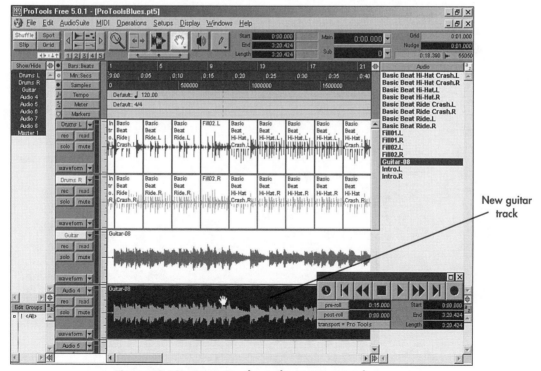

Figure 10.12   Dragging the audio to a new track.

Zoomer tool

Clicking tracks to zoom

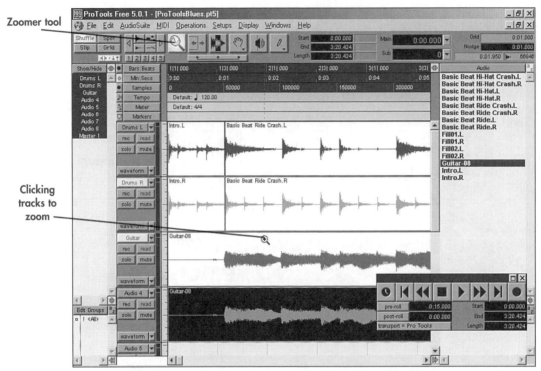

Figure 10.13   Zooming in on the tracks.

Slip button

Slipped slightly to the right

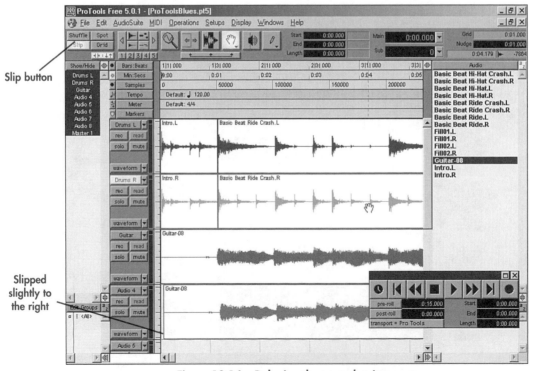

Figure 10.14   Delaying the second guitar part.

Pan values

Pan sliders

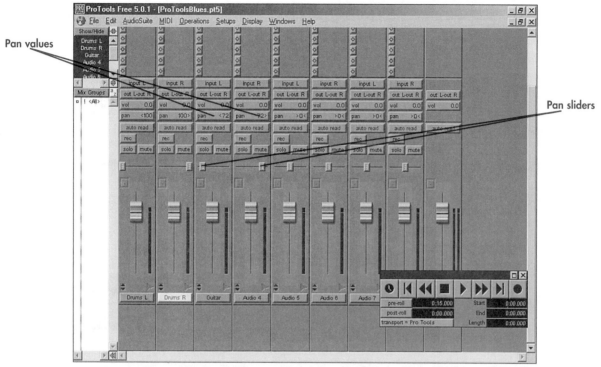

Figure 10.15   Delaying the second guitar part.

Dealing with Latency

Latency can be a big problem with computer-based studios, thanks to the time difference between a live sound and the one that's been processed through the computer. Software, after all, which isn't as fast as hardware devices, takes time to manipulate a sound. As you record tracks with Pro Tools, you'll probably notice this latency, and, in some cases, it'll drive you absolutely bonkers, with everything you try to record echoing.

One solution in Pro Tools is to decrease the size of the buffer used to store audio data. To do this, first select the Hardware entry in the Setups menu, as shown in Figure 10.16. When you do, the Hardware Setup dialog box appears (Figure 10.17). The setting you're interested in is H/W Buffer Size.

Click the H/W Buffer Size box to bring up the possible choices (Figure 10.18). The smaller you make this buffer, the less latency you'll experience. However, a small buffer means that your computer has to work harder to keep up with Pro Tools Free. If your system isn't powerful enough, you may have to increase the buffer size again. (If you see an error message telling you that the system has held off on interrupts too long, that's your signal to increase the buffer size.)

Another thing you can try, although it's never helped me much, is to give Pro Tools Free more processor power. You do this by changing the CPU Usage Limit setting, as shown in Figure 10.19.

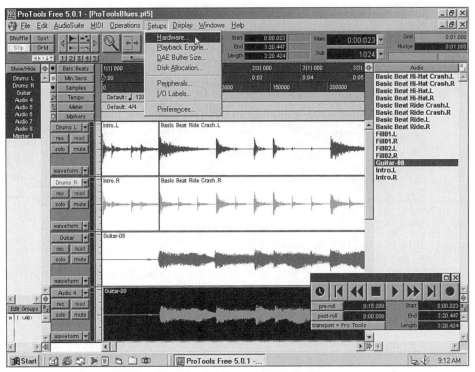

Figure 10.16   Choosing the Setup menu's Hardware command.

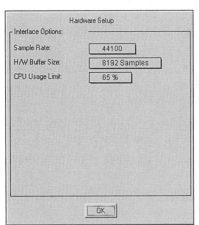

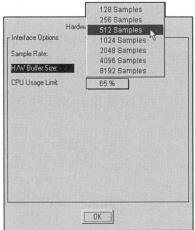

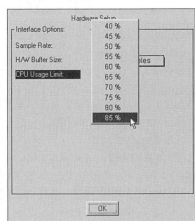

Figure 10.17   The Hardware Setup dialog box.

Figure 10.18   Choosing a buffer size.

Figure 10.19   Giving Pro Tools Free more CPU power.

If your computer just doesn't have the power to accept a small buffer and still keep up with Pro Tools Free, you'll have no choice but to live with the latency. You can, however, minimize its affect on your recordings. When overdubbing reduce the track's level to its minimum (Figure 10.20), which will prevent you from hearing that awful echo.

Notes from the Track Sheet

Pro Tools Free automatically remembers two level settings for each track: a playback level and a recording monitor level. When you toggle a track's Rec button, you may see the track's fader jump to a new setting. This is the level setting Pro Tools Free remembered for you.

Track's level

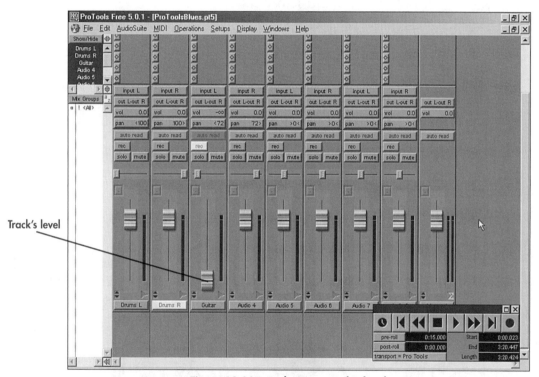

Figure 10.20   Reducing a track's level to 0.

The Least You Need to Know

◆ Punching-in is the process of rerecording a small part of a performance.

◆ Many recording systems provide automatic punching-in and punching-out.

◆ One way to keep different versions of a performance is to record each performance on a separate track.

◆ Another way to keep different versions of a performance is to use virtual tracks.

◆ Doubling is a common recording technique that creates big or omnipresent sounds.

◆ You can double tracks simply by playing and recording the same part a second time or by delaying a copy of a performance.

In This Part

Part 3

The Mixing Process

When the recording is done, you have a complete song in the form of a multitrack project. Unfortunately, home audio systems have no idea of how to play back such a project, so your last task is to take that multitrack project and turn it into a stereo mix. This task involves balancing the volume of each instrument, assigning each instrument a position in the stereo spectrum, and other important steps.

Here is also where you really dig into effects processors and learn to use them to turn out a professional-sounding mix. You learn to use EQ to smooth out the frequency content of your recordings, as well as use compressors to tame overly dynamic recordings. Reverb is another important tool that you need to learn to use judiciously.

By the end of this part, you will not only have learned everything you need to know to get started on your own recordings, but also have a short song called "Pro Tools Blues" that demonstrates all the techniques you've learned. This complete project not only demonstrates the proper use of recording and mixing tools, but also enables you to experiment with different mixes, including track volumes, effect settings, auxiliary sends, and more.

In This Chapter

◆ Understanding the stereo audio format

◆ Converting multitrack recordings to stereo

◆ Learning about the most common mixing tools

◆ Exploring software and hardware effects

Chapter 11

Introduction to Mixing

So now you've gotten all your song's tracks recorded. In a perfect world, you'd be done and could just plug your recording into the nearest CD player. Unfortunately, reality has other ideas. You now have eight or more tracks of music that need to be boiled down to stereo, which is only two tracks. Moreover, although you've employed every trick you've learned to make your tracks the best they can be, the tracks are still in pretty raw form. Taking these raw tracks and turning them into a song that the rest of the world can enjoy is all part of the art of mixing.

Multitrack vs. Stereo

Before you start mixing your song, you have to know what the point of mixing is, eh? Right now, you have a multitrack recording—possibly eight tracks or more—that have to be converted into a single stereo track. While this simplified statement might make the job sound easy, it's actually a lot more complicated than you probably imagine.

First of all, do you really know what stereo is? In its simplest form, stereo is nothing more than a special format of two-track recording. One track goes to your sound system's left channel and the other goes to the right, as shown in Figure 11.1.

The cool thing about stereo is that, even though there are only two channels, a sound can be emitted from anywhere in the stereo spectrum. Figure 11.2 shows what I mean. In the figure, you can see a stereo system that's playing back a recording by our favorite group, Willy Walnuts. The stereo spectrum reaches from the far left to the far right. The various instruments in the recording can be positioned anywhere between the two extremes.

Tracks

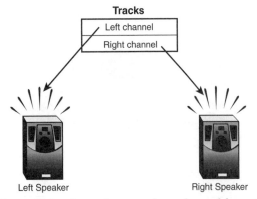

Figure 11.1 **Stereo is a two-channel sound format.**

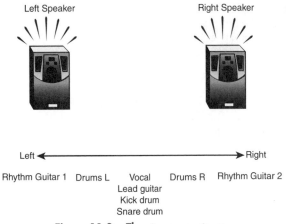

Figure 11.2 **The stereo spectrum.**

How does this stereo thing work? The stereo format relies on a few simple rules of physics:

1. If an identical sound comes from two sources at the same volume, the sound appears to be centered between the two sources.

2. If the sound becomes louder in the left source and quieter in the right, the sound seems to move toward the left.

3. If the sound becomes louder in the right source and quieter in the left, the sound seems to move toward the right.

That's the whole thing in a nutshell.

Notes from the Track Sheet

Now you know what those panning sliders do in Pro Tools Free or on other types of mixers. They simply change the relative left/right volume of a sound. When you move the pan slider to the left, the sound gets louder in the left speaker, and vice versa.

When mixing, your general goal is to take all those tracks you've recorded and assign them to a location in the stereo spectrum (Figure 11.3). The result then is a song in the stereo format, making the song playable on almost every home sound system on the planet, from a cheap boombox to a $10,000 home-theater system.

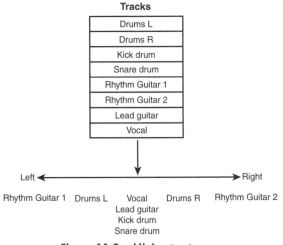

Figure 11.3 **Mixing to stereo.**

The Details

When mixing, you actually have a lot more to do than just position instruments in the stereo spectrum. You also have a last chance to polish your tracks to make them sound as pristine as possible. It's during mixing that you smooth out the relative volumes of each track, as well as add effects to make the final result sound more interesting and/or realistic.

Here's a list of tasks you'll probably complete as you mix your song:

◆ Pan each track to its appropriate position in the stereo spectrum.

◆ Adjust the volumes of each track to attain the proper balance between the instruments.

◆ Use EQ to fine-tune the tone of each track and to ensure each instrument has its own space in the mix.

◆ Use compressors and limiters to control the dynamics of a track so that it sits better in the mix.

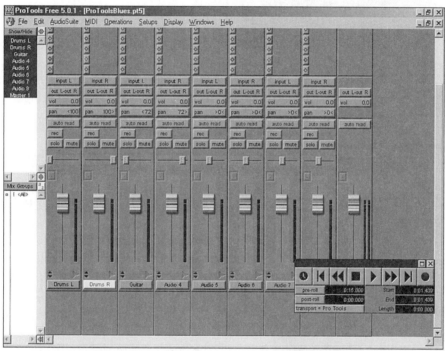

Figure 11.4   The mixer's panning and fader controls.

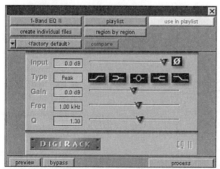

Figure 11.5   Pro Tools Free provides parametric EQ.

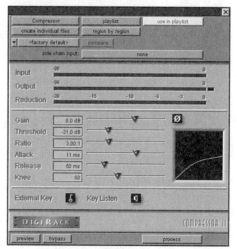

Figure 11.6   Compressors help smooth out sudden changes in volume.

◆ Use reverb where appropriate to add "space" to a track.

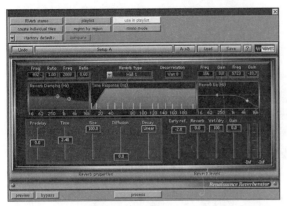

Figure 11.7 Reverb enables you to simulate the sound of various-sized rooms.

◆ Use digital delay to electronically double tracks.

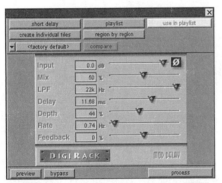

Figure 11.8 Using delay to spread a sound across the stereo spectrum is a common studio technique.

◆ Decorate the mix with interesting effects.

The Mixing Engineer's Tool Belt

Where are all the different tools you need to mix your song? That's a good question, the answer to which depends on your studio setup. Some tools, however, are so common that they're built right in to the main mixer. These tools include the following:

◆ Faders to adjust a track's volume

◆ Pan controls to adjust the location of a track in the stereo spectrum

◆ Parametric EQ to adjust a track's tone

◆ "Send" controls to send a copy of a track to a device or other track

Next, you'll be asking about effects, such as reverb, delay, and compression, right? In the case of Pro Tools Free and most other software-based recording systems, effects come in the form of *plug-ins*. Plug-ins are separate programs that "plug in" to your recording system, so that you can access them as if they were built in to the software.

Pro Tools Free comes with a full set of basic plug-ins, including EQ, compression, and delay (Figure 11.9). When you installed Pro Tools Free, all of these plug-ins were installed, as well. You can, however, purchase additional plug-ins to add to your system. In fact, to add reverb to your Pro Tools sessions, you'll have to purchase an additional plug-in. For some odd reason, Pro Tools Free doesn't come with reverb.

In the case of all-in-one workstations, effects are either built right in to the machine or can be purchased separately as circuit boards that you install in the machine. Figure 11.10 shows the Roland VS8F-2, which is an effects card for the Roland VS-series digital workstations and mixers.

Just Push Play

In almost all cases, you can purchase outboard effects, which are hardware effects units that you connect to whatever recording system you're using. You can purchase these units for prices ranging from around $100 up to many thousands of dollars. The average price for an effects unit for a home-base studio is $200 to $300.

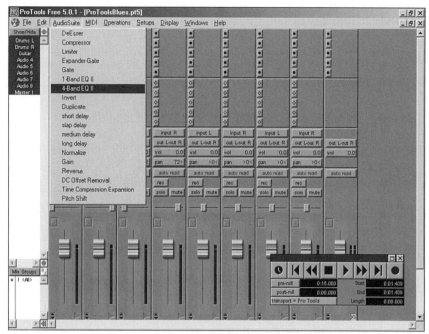

Figure 11.9   Pro Tools comes with a set of essential plug-in effects.

Figure 11.10   Roland effects card.

Now that you know a little about what mixing involves and about the tools you'll use to convert your multitrack recording into a stereo track, you're ready to get to work. You do that in the next chapter.

The Least You Need to Know

◆ Stereo is a special format of a two-track recording.

◆ Even though the stereo format provides only two channels, a sound can be emitted from anywhere in the stereo spectrum.

◆ When mixing, your general goal is to take all the tracks you've recorded and assign them to a location in the stereo spectrum.

◆ The most common tasks performed during mixing are volume adjustment, panning, tone adjustment, compression, and adding effects.

◆ Most effects for software-based recording systems come in the form of plug-ins.

◆ In the case of all-in-one workstations, effects are either built right in to the machine or can be purchased separately as circuit boards that you install in the machine.

In This Chapter

◆ Positioning instruments in a mix

◆ Balancing volumes between instruments

◆ Exploring the elements of a mix

◆ Creating mix groups

Chapter 12

Setting Up the Basic Mix

Although a professional mixing job requires a lot of knowledge and tons of equipment, the basic idea always is to condense your multiple tracks to the stereo format. This basic task involves adjusting the volume of each track, as well as assigning each track to a position in the stereo spectrum. Everything else that gets done in a mix is fine-tuning, polishing the basic mix until it sounds as good as possible. In this chapter, you learn to create the basic mix. The remaining chapters in this section deal with the details of fine-tuning your mix to perfection.

The Elements of a Basic Mix

Creating a basic stereo mix of your multitrack project is a relatively easy process. Just about anyone with a decent set of ears can set up their mix so that every instrument can be heard and each track in the project gets placed in a logical location in the stereo spectrum. In short, although mixing can be an intensely creative process, and allows plenty of room for personal taste and experimentation, certain tasks are almost always done in the tried-and-true way.

Position in a Stereo Mix

Standard rules dictate where instruments should appear in the stereo spectrum. Sure, skilled producers often break these rules. However, novice mixers need to stick with the tried and true. Keep the following rules in mind as you assemble your basic mix. Figure 12.1 illustrates the concept.

- Lead vocal, snare drum, kick drum, instrument solos, and bass guitar should usually be in the center.

- Overhead drum mics should be panned partially or fully left and right.

- Rhythm instruments such as guitar and keyboards should usually be panned to the sides.

- Stereo instruments should be panned partially or fully left or right.

- Background vocals can be in the center (combined with the lead vocal) or can be panned to the sides (to create wide, luscious vocal parts).

- Delayed copies of tracks should be panned opposite the original track (to create the illusion of an additional instrument) or panned in the same position as the original track (to create a "slap-back," echo type of effect).

Guitar Solo Delayed (25 ms)		Guitar Solo Delayed (35 ms)
Stereo Synth Left	Guitar Solo	Stereo Synth Right
	Bass Guitar	
Background vocal 1	Snare Drum	Background vocal 2
	Kick Drum	
Rhythm Guitar	Lead Vocal	Organ
Drum Overhead Left		Drum Overhead Right

Left Speaker   Right Speaker

Figure 12.1   Typical placement for instruments in a stereo mix.

Just Push Play

Keep in mind that, while the given rules work well for most situations and are suggested for your first forays into mixing, these rules are not cast in stone. Experienced mixing engineers come up with all sorts of wonderful ways to break the rules and create outstanding mixes that are works of art over and above the music contained in the mix. I strongly suggest that, as you continue to learn about mixing, you take the time to listen to and analyze a professionally mixed CD. Listen under headphones, because headphones really bring out the details by exaggerating the stereo spectrum.

Volume Balancing of Tracks

The next thing to consider is how loud each track should be. Attaining the perfect balance between the instruments and vocals can be trickier than you might think. This is because changing the volume of one track can have a profound effect on other tracks.

You might, for example, decide that the drums need to be louder. So you turn up the drums, only to discover that, while the vocal still sounds okay, the rhythm guitar is getting drowned out. So you increase the volume of the guitar, only to end up with the vocal hard to hear. And on and on. Anyone who's mixed a song is familiar with the infamous "volume creep." Before long, you've got everything turned way up and nothing sounds right. On top of that, the dog is howling and the next-door neighbor has called the police.

The solution to this problem (the volume, not the police) is to decide which elements of the mix are most important—that is, which tracks are the featured performances—and which others can be relegated to the background as support for the featured tracks. Not all tracks can be of equal volume. That's the fact, Jack!

But if you still end up heading for volume creep, turn down the louder tracks rather than turn up the quieter tracks. This technique prevents the overall mix from becoming too loud and peaking into distortion. Also, although compressor's can help tame a troublesome track, remember that you can manually change the volume of a track as you mix. Why waste a compressor on a track that just needs a level change once or twice in the mix?

Just Push Play

Here's a valuable hint: Just because you recorded a track, doesn't mean you have to use it. Sometimes you may find that taking a track out of a mix enables the mix to "breathe" better. Similarly, you may find that you can take a track out of an earlier part of a song, and then bring it back in later to give the mix an unexpected surprise or to keep an arrangement from getting stagnant and boring.

The Effects of Panning

To complicate matters, a track's position in the stereo spectrum—and even its tonal qualities—affects the perceived loudness of a track. Suppose, for example, you're stacking vocal tracks so that you have a three-part harmony panned to the center of the mix, as seen in Figure 12.2.

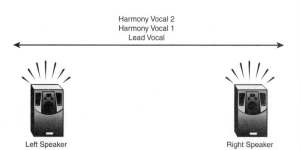

Harmony Vocal 2
Harmony Vocal 1
Lead Vocal

Left Speaker   Right Speaker

Figure 12.2   Stacking vocals in the center of a mix.

Now you decide that maybe you'd like to separate the vocals a little, so you pan one harmony to the left and the other to the right, as shown in Figure 12.3. Suddenly, the harmonies seem louder, just by the fact that they occupy different places in the stereo mix. At this point, the harmonies may even be drowning out the melody line and so need to be reduced in volume.

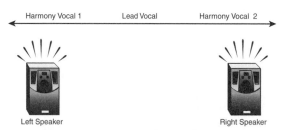

←— Harmony Vocal 1   Lead Vocal   Harmony Vocal 2 —→

Left Speaker   Right Speaker

Figure 12.3   Panning the vocals apart may increase their apparent volume.

As you see, panning is one important way to make an instrument more distinct in the mix. Panning similar-sounding tracks apart makes them seem louder, because they become more distinct. Using EQ to give instruments their own territory in the frequency range is another way to bring out an instrument, but you won't get to that until the following chapter.

Another thing to keep in mind is the way panning affects the cohesiveness of the instruments in a mix. By cohesiveness, I mean the way the elements of the mix work together. Specifically, the closer you position instruments in the stereo spectrum, the more they seem to occupy the same space, as if they were recorded at the same time in the same room. On the other hand, when you pan instruments to the extreme left and right, they get separated from the rest of the mix and become more distinct. Just panning such tracks back a little ways toward the middle makes them blend better with the rest of the instruments. Of course, such choices amount to taste and the effect you want to create.

Notes from the Track Sheet

One of the most amazing producers on the planet, Roy Thomas Baker, is an expert at not only breaking the rules, but building mixes so complex that every time you listen, you hear something new. The 1970s progressive-rock band Queen is probably Baker's most famous client. Listen to the albums *Sheer Heat Attack* and *Night at the Opera* to hear some truly astonishing mixing jobs—especially the magnificent "Bohemian Rhapsody."

Roy Thomas Baker is probably my favorite producer of all time—one of my heroes, for sure. On this book's disc, I've included a song titled "She's Tall Enough," where I attempted to pull off a sort of RTB production. Just the song's introduction was a huge amount of work, as you'll learn when you read the song's accompanying case history. My meager attempt gave me even more respect for the work RTB must have put into Queen's albums.

Exploring Pro Tools Blues

Since the previous chapter, I've been busy working on "Pro Tools Blues," adding tracks and setting up a basic mix. You'll find the Pro Tools session for the song on this book's disc, in the Chapter12\ProToolsBlues12_1 folder. Load it up and give it a listen. The mix, which is pretty basic at this point, is illustrated in Figure 12.4. Put on headphones and listen closely to the song. Try to pinpoint all the elements of the mix shown in the illustration.

When you've located all of the instruments in the mix, take some time to analyze what you hear. Are there, perhaps, elements of the mix

that need to change? For example, could the rhythm guitar be turned up a little? Listen again and think about it. Sometimes, the rhythm guitar is barely audible, usually when the lead guitar pops in. A good example of this is right at the beginning of the song.

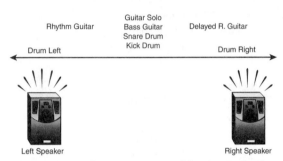

Figure 12.4   The current state of the Pro Tools Blues mix.

On the other hand, when the lead guitar is out of the picture, you can hear the rhythm guitar clearly. Does this mean that, instead of the rhythm guitar being too quiet, maybe the lead guitar is too loud?

The rhythm guitar has a greater effect on the song than you might think, even when you can barely hear it. To see what I mean, set the song back to the beginning by clicking the Return to Zero button in the Transport window. Then click the Play button. As you listen to the lead guitar in the beginning, click the Mute buttons on the two rhythm guitar tracks, as shown in Figure 12.5. Whoa! That rhythm guitar really does make a big difference, even when it's not right up front in the mix. This experiment demonstrates how support instruments don't have to be loud to do their job. Often, less is more.

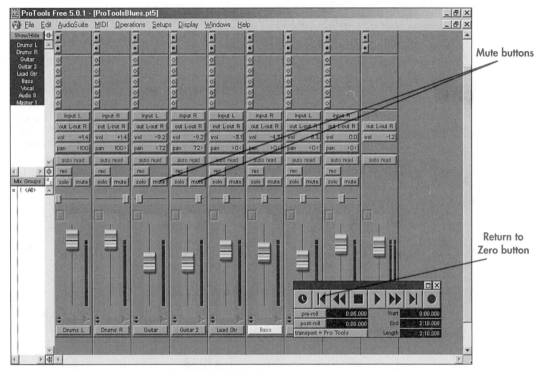

Mute buttons

Return to
Zero button

Figure 12.5   Muting the rhythm guitar tracks.

So is the rhythm guitar too low or not? Let's do some work on the mix and see what happens. Specifically, turn up the rhythm guitar a little. Remember that you'll want to turn up both the rhythm guitar and its delayed copy, as shown in Figure 12.6, so that the sound of the guitar stays balanced left to right in the mix. Try a setting of –6.2 for both channels, as shown in the figure.

At a setting of –6.2, the rhythm guitar is more defined in the mix, but still stays in the background where it belongs. Notice that the lead guitar now doesn't sound quite as loud. This is an example of how changing one level affects the others. The rhythm guitar has gained a little more dominance in the mix, so the lead guitar seems quieter.

The drums are affected by the change, too, although the effect is less noticeable on the kick drum, because the kick drum's sound is very different from the sound of the guitars. (Or in technical terms, the kick drum occupies a different area of the frequency range. You learn about this stuff in the next chapter when you fiddle with EQ.) The same is true of the bass guitar, which stays down there with the kick drum.

You may be wondering what those level-setting numbers mean. The level settings for each track are measured in *decibels*, which is abbreviated *dB*. When you set a fader to 0.0 dB, the channel's level is exactly the same as the level of the recording associated with the channel. That is, the level is neither turned up nor turned down. Decibel settings below 0 (lower volume) are shown as negative values, whereas values above 0 (higher volume) are shown as positive values. Figure 12.7 shows Pro Tools's faders set to various levels.

Set the levels to –6.2

Move the faders up

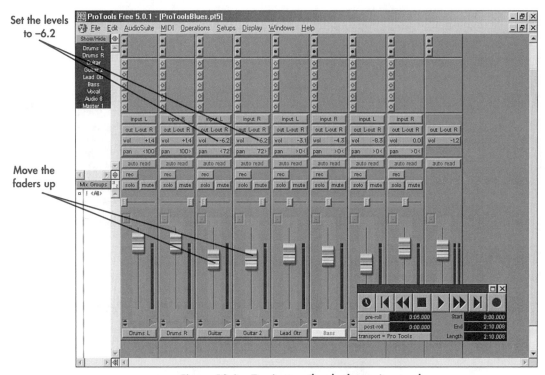

Figure 12.6   Turning up the rhythm guitar tracks.

Fader set to 0.0 db

Fader set to a decrease of –8.0 db

Fader set to an increase of +3.0 db

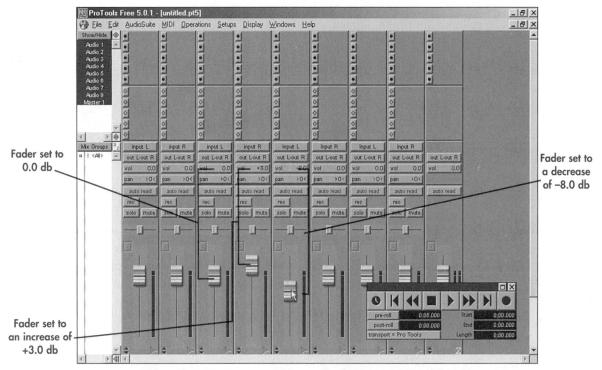

Figure 12.7   Faders set to different level settings, measured in dB.

Getting back to "Pro Tools Blues," while you're fiddling with the mix, try panning tracks to different locations and listen to how such changes affect the song. How does it sound, for example, to pan both rhythm guitar tracks (the original and the delayed) all the way to the left and right (Figure 12.8), instead of only partially left and right. I think you'll find that the rhythm guitar part becomes even more prominent in the mix.

Now try panning both rhythm guitar tracks all the way to the left and the lead guitar all the way to the right, as shown in Figure 12.9. How does it sound? Now that the original rhythm guitar track and its delayed copy are both panned to the same place, the guitar sounds like it has a very slight echo. The lead guitar, on the other hand, is well defined on the right, but seems less important, because it's no longer front and center.

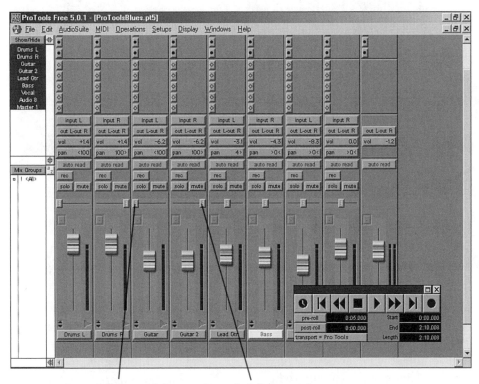

Panned all the way left   Panned all the way right

Figure 12.8   The rhythm tracks panned far left and right.

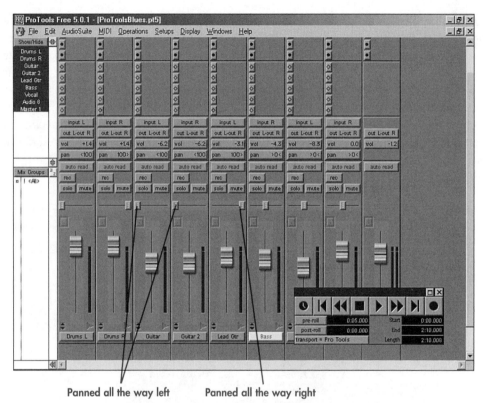

Panned all the way left   Panned all the way right

Figure 12.9   The rhythm tracks panned far left and right.

Grouping Tracks

If you think that there ought to be an easier way to handle stereo tracks like our drums or paired tracks like our rhythm guitar and its matching delayed copy, you're right. I mean, why, for example, should you have to worry about getting the volume of the left and right pair of a stereo track perfectly balanced? The machine should handle that for you. Most recording systems enable you to group tracks so that they can be manipulated as a single entity.

To see what I mean, let's group the rhythm guitar tracks so that they're easier to manage. Follow these steps:

1. Click the Guitar button under the third track's fader (see Figure 12.10). The button lights.

2. Hold down the Shift key on your keyboard, and click the Guitar 2 button under the fourth track's fader (see Figure 12.10). That button lights, too.

3. Click the Mix Groups button, as shown in Figure 12.10. The Mix Groups menu pops up.

4. Select the New Group command, as shown in Figure 12.11. The New Group dialog box appears.

5. In the Name for Group box, type Rhythm Guitar (Figure 12.12).

6. Click the OK button to create the group. Pro Tools adds group indicators to the tracks, as shown in Figure 12.13.

The Mix
Groups button

The Guitar
button

The Guitar 2
button

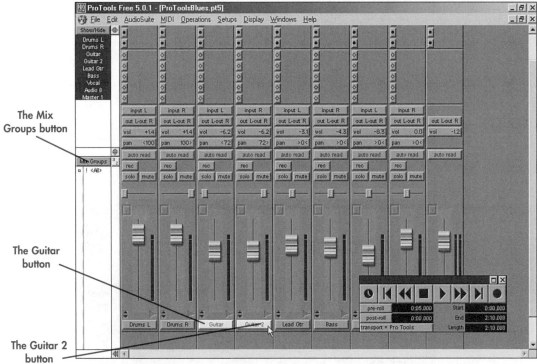

Figure 12.10   The buttons needed to create the guitar mix group.

Figure 12.11   The Mix Group menu.

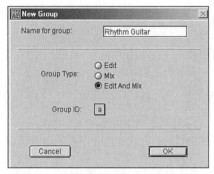

Figure 12.12   Naming the mix group.

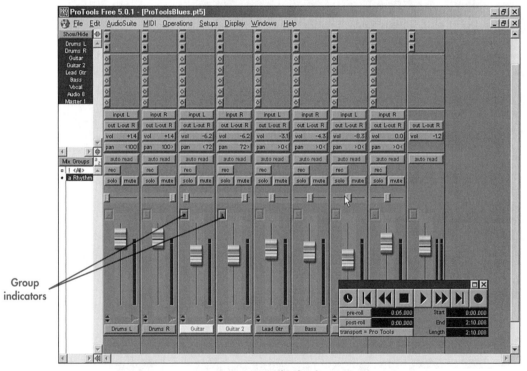

Figure 12.13   The final mix group.

Now that you have your group created, move the track 3 fader, and the track 4 fader moves with it. Cool! The same is true of the Mute buttons; click one of them, and Pro Tools instantly mutes both tracks. You can place as many tracks as you want into a group. For now, though, create a second group, named Drums, for the first and second tracks. Now you can easily change the volume of the drums, being sure that both

the left and right drum channels stay balanced. In the Chapter12\ProToolsBlues12_2 folder of this book's CD, you'll find the ProToolsBlues session with all these changes in place.

As you can see … well, maybe *hear* would be the better word … just balancing track volumes and panning instruments goes a long way toward building your final mix. As I said before, these tasks are the most important in the mixing process, because it squeezes down all those tracks you recorded into the stereo format. In the next couple chapters, you learn the studio tricks that can turn your raw tracks into a polished production.

The Least You Need to Know

◆ Lead vocal, snare drum, kick drum, instrument solos, and bass guitar should usually be in the center of a mix.

◆ Stereo tracks, such as overhead drum mics, should be panned partially or fully left and right, as should rhythm instruments such as guitar and keyboards.

◆ Changing the volume of one track can have a profound affect on other tracks.

◆ You need to decide which elements of the mix are most important and which others can be relegated to the background as support for the featured tracks.

◆ Panning similar sounding tracks apart makes them seem louder because it makes them more distinct.

◆ Mix groups enable you to manipulate multiple tracks as a single entity.

In This Chapter

◆ Understanding the frequency spectrum

◆ Exploring different types of equalizers

◆ Applying EQ to a mix

◆ Placing instruments in their own sonic space

Using Equalizers

"Pro Tools Blues" is actually starting to sound like a real song. As far as tracks go, it's still missing the vocals, but that's only because I wanted to save the vocals for a lesson on using compressors. In case it isn't obvious from the chapter titles, that's one of the things you'll be doing in the next chapter. Here, you learn to use EQ to manipulate the tonal quality of tracks, a task that can be as meticulous as it is important.

Using Equalizers

Believe it or not, you've been using a simple form of equalizer ever since you played your first CD (or record, for those of us who have been around a while). Let me explain. You know how when you're listening to a CD, sometimes things don't sound quite right? Maybe the bass is a little weak or the treble is too harsh. So you spin those bass and treble tone controls until the CD sounds the way you like it. What you've just done is increase or decrease the volume of certain frequencies, which is exactly what an equalizer does.

The main difference between an equalizer and the tone controls on your stereo is flexibility. An equalizer lets you zero in on specific ranges of frequencies, whereas a tone control on your stereo is preset to a frequency range. Usually, the bass control on a stereo system boosts all the frequencies below a specific point, and the treble control boosts all the frequencies above a specific point.

Want an example or two? Figure 13.1 shows what your stereo system's frequency response might look like in a perfect world. Of course, this isn't a perfect world, so no machine's frequency response is going to be so flat. The figure graphs decibels (sort of like volume) vertically and graphs frequency horizontally. So the higher the decibel value for a frequency, the louder the frequency is. Get it? In the figure then, every frequency has exactly the same level, which is 0 dB.

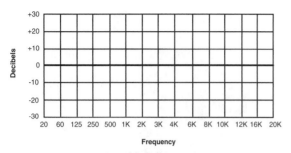

Figure 13.1   Flat frequency response.

Now, what happens when you crank up the bass control on your receiver? Figure 13.2 shows the probable result. How high the low frequencies go depends on how far up you crank the bass. Go ahead and rattle the windows! Notice, in the figure, the way all the low frequencies go up, creating a kind of shelf. This could be why they refer to such a frequency control as a *shelving EQ*. (Duh!)

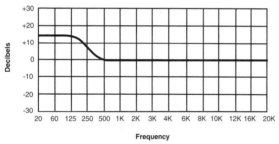

Figure 13.2   Increasing the bass.

Now that we've got the bass up enough to rattle the windows, let's turn up the treble enough to make your cats yowl. When you do that, your frequency graph will probably look something like Figure 13.3. Notice that we've got another shelf, this time at the high end. Yep, the treble control on your stereo acts as shelving EQ, too.

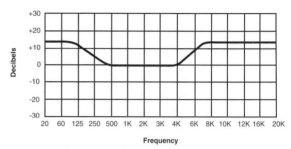

Figure 13.3   Increasing the treble.

Some stereo systems have, beside bass and treble controls, a midrange control, which enables you to boost or cut the middle frequencies. If your receiver has such a control, and you crank it up, the graph in Figure 13.4 shows what the frequencies might look like. What if you turn down one of the tone controls? Figure 13.5 shows a frequency graph for a stereo system whose bass control has been turned down.

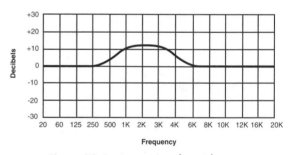

Figure 13.4   Increasing the midrange.

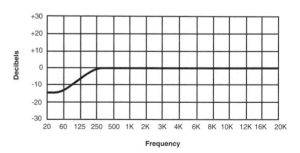

Figure 13.5   Cutting the bass.

As I said before, increased high frequencies make cats yowl. No, wait! What I said before was that, unlike the tone controls on your stereo system, an equalizer—or EQ as us cool musicians call them—can zero in on narrower frequency areas, called *frequency bands*. For example, suppose you decide the hi-hat in your drum recording could be a little brighter. You might EQ the track around 4K, as shown in Figure 13.6.

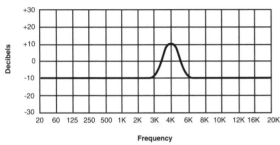

Figure 13.6   EQ'ing a frequency band around 4K.

You can see in the figure that the frequency band affected by EQ'ing a track at 4K is much narrower than the frequency band affected by the midrange tone control on a stereo system. This is what makes EQ so valuable and powerful. Notice how the target frequency, 4K, is in the center of the boosted region, with lower and higher frequencies being affected less and less as you move away from the target frequency.

The width of this "hump" in the frequency graph is referred to as *bandwidth*, or more technically as *Q*. Some equalizers let you not only choose the center frequency of a band, but also the bandwidth (called Q, remember?).

EQ Plug-Ins

Take a gander at Figure 13.7, which shows one of the cool Pro Tools plug-ins you can get from Waves (www.waves.com). Right now, the EQ is set for flat frequency response, which is why the plug-in's display looks a lot like my Figure 13.1.

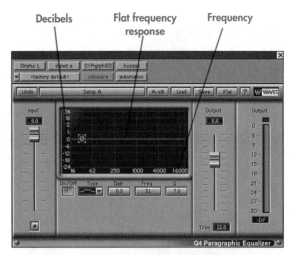

Figure 13.7   An EQ plug-in.

So let's see how we might use this tool to change the tone of a track. This particular plug-in is insanely easy to use. All you have to do is drag the marker on the frequency line to change the frequency curve. Figure 13.8 shows the EQ set to provide a boost at around 1000 Hz, or what those aforementioned cool musicians call 1K. Notice the displays for gain, frequency, and Q. If you need a reminder, gain is the amount of boost or cut, frequency is the frequency around which the gain is applied, and Q is the bandwidth.

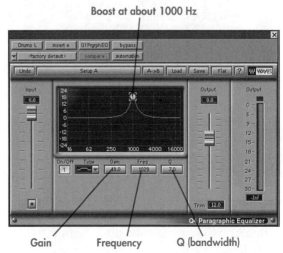

Figure 13.8   Boosting at around 1000 Hz.

To understand Q better, compare Figures 13.9 and 13.10. The first shows an EQ set to a wide bandwidth, whereas the second figure shows a very narrow bandwidth. You can see that changing the value of Q changes the width of the frequencies affected by the cut or gain.

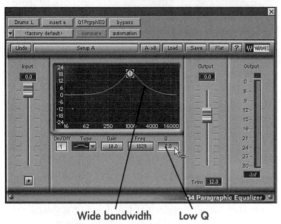

Wide bandwidth   Low Q

Figure 13.9   Low Q creates a wide bandwidth.

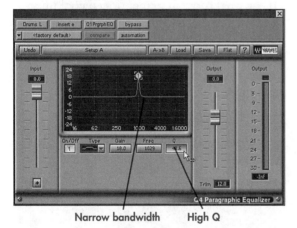

Narrow bandwidth   High Q

Figure 13.10   High Q creates a narrow bandwidth.

Multiband EQs

So far, you've been looking at an EQ that manages only a single band of frequencies. Most parametric EQs can handle three or four frequencies, and some go way beyond even that. Figure 13.11, for example, shows another Waves EQ plug-in. This one enables you to

manipulate eight different frequency bands. Of course, a plug-in like this sucks up a lot more computer-processor power than the single-band version does, so it must be used judiciously. If you need to EQ this many frequencies, there must be something really wrong with your recording.

Just Push Play

When you're recording, you need to position the mic just right to get an instrument's best sound. If you find yourself spinning a lot of EQ controls in order to get a good recorded sound, you probably need to reposition your mic.

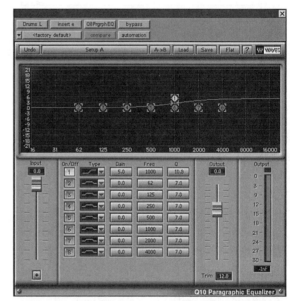

Figure 13.11   This parametric EQ can manage eight frequency bands simultaneously.

Pro Tools Free and EQ

Now I'm sure you're wondering if you're going to have to go out and buy the Waves plug-ins to have EQ in your Pro Tools Free projects. The answer is no. I used the Waves plug-ins as examples because they display a frequency graph of how the EQ is being applied. Pro Tools Free comes with its own set of EQ plug-ins, one of which is shown in Figure 13.12. As you can see, this is a four-band EQ. The high and low frequencies are managed with shelving EQ and so have no need of a Q control. The other two sets of EQ controls include gain, frequency, and Q.

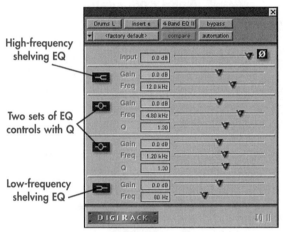

High-frequency shelving EQ

Two sets of EQ controls with Q

Low-frequency shelving EQ

Figure 13.12   One EQ plug-in that comes with Pro Tools Free.

Applying EQ

In concept, EQ is easy to understand. It's not, however, easy to apply unless you know what frequencies to manipulate. It also helps to know what a well-recorded instrument sounds like. The only way to really learn this stuff is by experimenting and getting some experience, not to mention listening to professional recordings.

I can't give you years of experience (if I could, I'd keep all that experience for myself, anyway), but I can get you started. Load up the most recent "Pro Tools Blues" project, and we'll start experimenting with EQ. The first step is to add an EQ plug-in to the track with which you want to work. We'll start with the drums.

Take a look at Figure 13.13. See the small buttons, the ones with the black circles, above the drum tracks? These buttons, called *insert buttons*, are where you insert plug-ins for the tracks. As you can see, all the tracks have insert buttons, but we're only concerned with the drum tracks right now.

Insert buttons

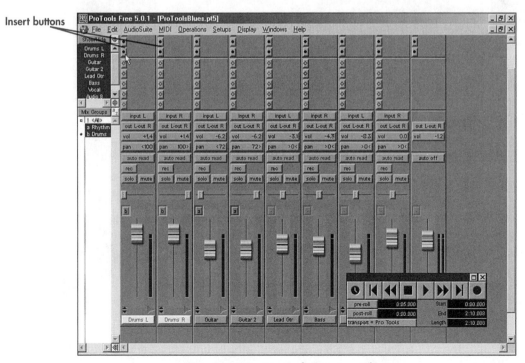

Figure 13.13   Pro Tools Free insert buttons.

Click one of the insert buttons on the first drum track, and a small menu appears. Choose the Plug-In command, and all the Pro Tools Free plug-ins appear, as shown in Figure 13.14. Select the 1-Band EQ plug-in, also as shown in the figure.

When you select the plug-in, it appears on the screen, as shown in Figure 13.15. The plug-in features five main controls, as well as five types of EQ, as labeled in the figure. Here's what those controls do:

- ◆ **Input.** Used to adjust level to avoid clipping
- ◆ **Type.** Used to select the type of EQ
- ◆ **Gain.** Used to cut or boost the level of selected frequencies

- ◆ **Freq.** Used to select the frequency band to manipulate
- ◆ **Q.** Used to set the bandwidth affected by the EQ

Notes from the Track Sheet

You're already familiar with low-shelf, high-shelf, and peak types of EQ, but what the heck is that high-pass and low-pass stuff? Thankfully, you've asked an easy question. (This is one of the advantages of being a writer and being able to make up the questions you ask. You just can't stump me!) A low-pass filter allows only low frequencies to get through, and a high-pass filter—bet you can guess this one—allows only high frequencies to get through.

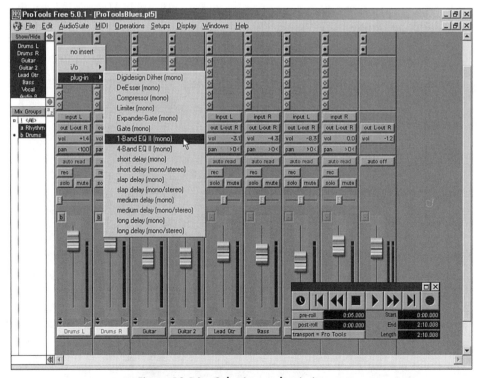

Figure 13.14   Selecting a plug-in insert.

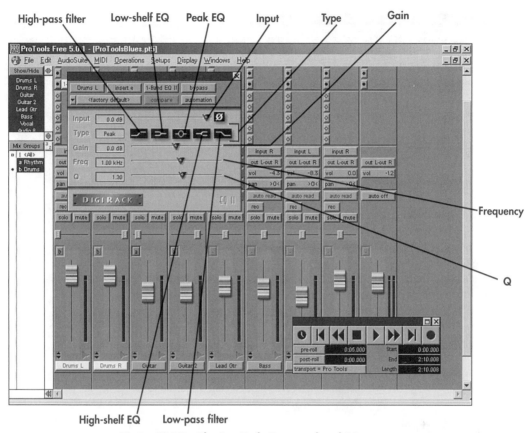

Figure 13.15   The Pro Tools Free one-band EQ.

So now that we have an EQ on the drums, let's start experimenting. (Because the drum tracks are part of a mix group, the EQ affects both tracks equally. That is, you don't need to put an EQ on the other drum track.) First, we need to solo the drum tracks. To do this, click the Solo button on the first drum track. Because the drum tracks are in their own mix group, Pro Tools solos both tracks. You can tell because the Solo buttons light up. Notice that, on all other tracks, the Mute buttons come on. That's what solo does: turns off every track except the one you're soloing.

Now, click the Play button in the Transport window. As the drums play, listen closely to

kick drum. Train yourself to focus on it, ignoring the other drum sounds. Got it? This is a skill that'll be very helpful to you as you evaluate more and more complex mixes. You need to be able to see the trees, as well as the forest.

Just Push Play

Remember that when you boost EQ, you increase the volume of the selected frequencies, which means the sound coming from your speakers gets louder. For this reason, keep your monitoring system at a safe level when applying "additive" EQ.

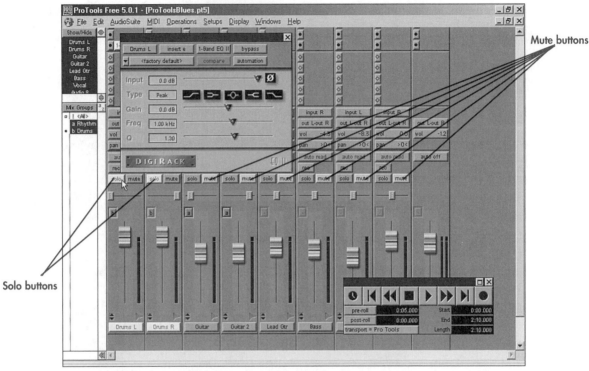

Figure 13.16   The Solo and Mute buttons.

EQ'ing a Kick Drum

Now stop the playback, and set the gain control on the EQ all the way up to 12.0 dB. Also set the frequency to about 50 Hz. Leave the Q where it is. Figure 13.17 shows these new EQ settings.

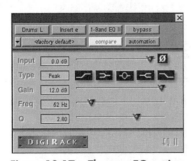

Figure 13.17   The new EQ setting.

See the Bypass button in the upper-right corner of the EQ? Click it. Now the EQ is set the way we want it, but it is off. Start playing back the drums again. Focus on the kick drum, and then turn off the Bypass button, which turns on the EQ. Hear the difference? The frequencies down around 40 to 60 Hz are where that deep bass lives. Hip-hop producers just love that stuff. Figure 13.18 shows the frequency graph for this setting.

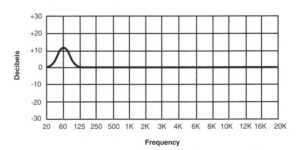

Figure 13.18   Boosting the kick drum 12 dB at 60 Hz.

Notes from the Track Sheet

Because our drum tracks are already mixed in stereo, you can't isolate one drum from another. Keep in mind that all the EQ you apply affects all the drums as a whole. However, changes have different effects on different drums. For example, changes in low frequencies have no effect on cymbals, because cymbals have no energy down there. On the other hand, changes in the low frequencies do affect tom-toms, but not as much as they do the kick drum.

Now raise the frequency to about 150 Hz. At 150 Hz, the kick drum should have more thump, the kind of stuff that, when it's loud enough, seems to pound your chest. Figure 13.19 shows the graph for this setting. Now raise the frequency to about 3K. This is about where you might find the slap of the beater against the drum head. Figure 13.20 shows the graph for this setting.

EQ'ing a Snare Drum

Snare drums have no energy down where you first boosted the kick drum. That is, changes in the 60 Hz range won't change the sound of the snare much. The first useful area is around 300 Hz, where you can add or remove some "pop" from the snare drum. Go ahead and set your drum EQ to about 300 Hz, and listen, this time focusing on the snare drum. Hear what I mean by pop?

Now try boosting somewhere between 1 KHz and 2 KHz. This adds a lot of grunge to the sound. At about 4 KHz, you can bring out the rattle of the snares, whereas at about 8 KHz, you add some high-end "sizzle." Go ahead and try it.

EQ'ing Cymbals

The frequency range for cymbals is way up there, although they do have some energy in the lower highs, such as around 2 KHz. EQ'ing at 4 KHz to 6 KHz brings out the brightness of instruments with high-end energy, whereas EQ'ing at around 10 KHz affects the very high sizzle. You should now know how to use the EQ plug-in, so go ahead and experiment with these and other frequencies while listening to the affect on the cymbals. Figure 13.21 shows a boost in the very high end.

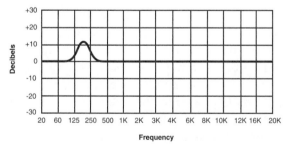

Figure 13.19   Boosting the kick drum 12 dB at 150 Hz.

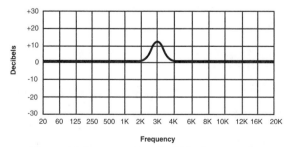

Figure 13.20   Boosting the kick drum 12 dB at 3 KHz.

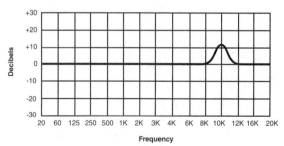

Figure 13.21   Boosting the cymbals 12 dB at 10 KHz.

Notes from the Track Sheet

Sorry for the use of such vague terms as slap, pop, rattle, and sizzle, but no one has ever come up with actual terms for the sounds you get when fiddling with EQ. This can lead to confusion when a producer tells an engineer something like, "How about adding some air to the cymbals, getting rid of some grit on the snare drum, and fattening up the bass?" Luckily, a good engineer can translate this mumbo jumbo into "Boost the cymbals at 12 KHz, cut the snare at 1 KHz, and boost the bass at 100 Hz." Or something like that.

EQ'ing Bass Guitar

Now, let's move on to the bass guitar. First you need to turn off soloing on the drum tracks (click the Solo button on the first drum track), and then turn on soloing for the bass guitar track.

You also need to insert an EQ plug-in on the bass track, but let's first get rid of the one on the drums. On the drum track, click the small button to the left of the plug-in's name. (This is the same button you clicked to add the insert.) When the menu appears, select No Insert. The insert vanishes from the track.

Now, add a one-band EQ to the bass track. Set the gain to 12 dB and the frequency to 60 Hz.

Notes from the Track Sheet

You didn't really need to remove the EQ from the drum track before placing one on the bass track. You can use as many EQ plug-ins as you want. Sort of. Each plug-in uses some of your computer's calculating power, so you should always use as few as possible. Don't leave them in tracks because you're lazy like me. (You couldn't get me off the couch with a flamethrower.)

The bass track will be a lot easier to experiment with, because the track contains nothing but the bass guitar, unlike the drums which were already mixed together in stereo. Start by listening to changes in the 60 Hz range. Just as with the kick drum, the bass guitar's deep bass is in this region, with around 200 Hz being the solid bass. Around the 2K range, you can add presence to the bass, helping it cut through the mix.

EQ'ing Guitar

An electric guitar has a fairly wide range of frequencies to fiddle with. Usually, however, you want to avoid cranking up the low end (around 150 Hz), which will cause the guitar to compete with the bass, as well as make the whole mix muddy. A guitar has a lot of midrange content in the 600 Hz to 2 KHz range. At the low end of this range, you get a sound a lot like you get with a wah-wah pedal rocked all the way back. In the upper part of this range, you get what they call "bite," and around 4 KHz, you get the guitar's high end. Above 6 KHz, you're not going to find much going on.

Let's experiment with the rhythm guitar track in "Pro Tools Blues." First you need to turn off soloing on the bass track, and then turn on soloing for the rhythm guitar track. You also need to remove the insert from the bass track, and add an EQ plug-in on the guitar track. You know how to do this, right? When you're set up with a guitar EQ, go ahead and experiment with the different frequencies, especially the ones I mentioned. Remember to use the Bypass button to compare the unprocessed track with the EQ'ed one.

EQ'ing Vocals

The human voice occupies a surprisingly large area of the frequency spectrum and often competes with instruments such as guitar, drums, organ, and so on. Because the vocal is usually the centerpiece of your song, you want to make extra sure that it stands out properly. The best way to do this is to use *subtractive EQ* (turning down gain, rather than up) to remove frequencies from any competing instruments. This process is kind of like cutting a hole in which you can place the vocal.

Every voice is different, not to mention separated into male and female (on this planet, anyway), so it's nearly impossible to provide rules for EQ'ing. Keep in mind, however, that the human voice has a lot of energy in the 4 KHz range, and you might want to start there when trying to bring the vocal more forward in the mix. A little EQ in the 4 KHz range can help you avoid having to increase the vocal's volume.

Currently, "Pro Tools Blues" has no vocal tracks. If you want to experiment with vocal EQ, make a copy of the project and then add your own vocal track. I'll be adding my vocal track in the next chapter, when we talk about compression.

Notes from the Track Sheet

Most professional engineers and producers will tell you that, rather than rely on EQ, you should get the best possible sound while you're recording. EQ can never turn a bad sound into a good one; it can only improve it some. It's kind of like polishing a diamond. If you try the same thing with a hunk of sandstone, all the polishing in the world won't help much.

The Tricky Part of EQ'ing

So far in this chapter, we've looked at using EQ to improve the tonal qualities of single tracks. The truth is, however, that the way a track sounds when it's soloed is not necessarily the way it should sound in a finished mix. In

fact, if you were to have an opportunity to examine a professional engineer's work, you might be astounded to find a couple of tracks that sound wonderful in the full mix, but sound horrible when soloed.

Most Important!

The most important reason to use EQ is to make a track sound better in the full mix. After all, this is the only way most people will hear it. How the track sounds when it's soloed is pretty much irrelevant, although it's not a bad start toward building your final mix.

Once you get your tracks sounding the way you like when soloed, listen carefully to how they sound all together. You may find, for example, that the guitar's low end is making it hard to hear the bass or is making the mix seem to rumble. In a case like this, EQ the guitar while listening to the entire mix. You should be able to not only remove annoying rumble, but also separate the guitar sound from the bass sound. Sure the guitar will sound thinner when soloed. So what?

Everything in Its Place

The bottom line is that every instrument in your mix should have its own area in the frequency spectrum and should avoid encroaching on another track's areas whenever possible. This goal is not 100 percent attainable, because many tracks, such guitar and drums, share areas in the frequency spectrum. However, just manipulating different frequencies of overlapping tracks can make a big difference in your mix.

For sure, you need to avoid allowing tracks to encroach in places where they don't belong, such as with our guitar and bass example. The law here is that similar frequencies tend to mask each other. A good example is two people talking at the same time. It can be pretty hard to follow the conversation, because the voices tend to blend into one sound. If someone else in the room rings a bell, you can hear the bell clearly, in spite of the babbling of our two inconsiderate conversationalists.

In this case of voices and bells, your ears hear two distinct sounds: people yakking and a bell ringing. You hear the bell clearly because it has much more high-frequency content than human voices do, and so fits into a different area of the frequency spectrum, even though some of the bell's sound may overlap the frequency of the voices.

EQ and All-in-One Workstations

EQ is such as important part of the recording and mixing process that virtually every workstation and mixer comes with some sort of EQ. On a standard mixer, every channel usually has at least a two-band EQ, and often a three- or four-band EQ. On an analog mixer, you control the EQ with knobs on each channel, as shown in Figure 13.22.

EQ section, three knobs
for each chanel
Figure 13.22   EQ on a small analog mixer.

Digital mixers, including those found on all-in-one workstations, may or may not have knobs for EQ. The more inexpensive units rarely do. Often, you control EQ (and other settings) on the machine's LCD screen. Figure 13.23, for example, shows the Tascam 788 Digital Portastudio's controls.

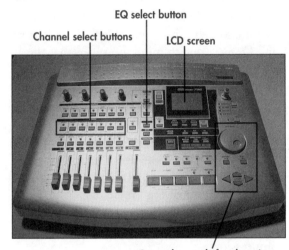

Figure 13.23   EQ'ing on the Tascam 788.

On this machine, you press a button to select the track on which you want to work. You then press another button to select the function (in this case EQ), and then use the general controls to change values in the LCD screen. Figure 13.24 shows the 788's screen when it's set up for EQ.

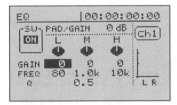

Figure 13.24   The Tascam 788's EQ screen.

EQ and "Pro Tools Blues"

This chapter includes yet another version of "Pro Tools Blues," this one with some EQ'ing done. Load this project, which you'll find in the Chapter13\ProToolsBlues13 directory, and listen to the song's current state. Following is a list of the EQ'ing choices I made. While listening, keep these changes in mind, and don't be afraid to use the Bypass button on the EQ plug-ins to make before and after comparisons. Here's what I did:

◆ Drums are EQ'ed –8 dB at 62 Hz to tame the kick drum a little. I thought the "thump" was too heavy.

◆ Rhythm guitar EQ'ed +6 dB at 5 KHz to give it a little high-end "shimmer."

◆ Lead guitar EQ'ed with low-shelf, –3.5 dB at 150 Hz. This is to take away some low-end competition with the bass guitar.

◆ Lead guitar also EQ'ed –7 dB at 1 KHz with a low Q (wide bandwidth) of 0.71. I thought the guitar had too much bite and was harsh on the ears. The wide bandwidth lets me get a bigger chunk of frequencies centered around 1 KHz.

◆ Bass guitar EQ'ed –2 dB at 140 Hz, because I thought it was a little too boomy.

And that's it. Listen close and see whether you agree with my EQ choices. To some extent, it's a matter of taste, with the ultimate goal getting the entire mix to sound as good as possible.

If all this sounds a little overwhelming, it's only because it is. Learning to EQ is one of those things you can do only through experience. A book like this can get you started, but your ears have to know what they're hearing and how to interpret changes you make. You can completely destroy a mix by using EQ improperly. Scared yet? Wait until next chapter, when we talk about compressors! Then you'll know the true meaning of fear. (Just kidding. Sort of.)

The Least You Need to Know

◆ The bandwidth affected by an equalizer is called Q.

◆ The frequencies down around 40 to 60 Hz are where that deep bass lives, whereas around 150 Hz is the solid, thumping bass.

◆ Around 300 Hz you can find the "pop" of the snare drum, whereas around 4 KHz you might find the rattle of the snares.

◆ Around 1 KHz to 2 KHz is where you can find some grunge or bite.

◆ EQ'ing at 4 KHz to 6 KHz brings out the brightness of instruments with high-end energy, whereas EQ'ing at around 10 KHz affects the very high sizzle.

◆ The most important reason to use EQ is to make a track sound better in the full mix.

In This Chapter

- ◆ Learning about audio waveforms
- ◆ Understanding limiting and compression
- ◆ How to apply limiting and compression
- ◆ When to use limiting and compression

Chapter 14

Using Compressors and Limiters

Ready to get your thinking cap cooking? Compressors are probably the hardest sonic tool in your recording arsenal to understand, but they are invaluable for creating professional-sounding recordings. The thing about compressors is that their effects are often hard to hear. In fact, once you do hear a compressor working, you've probably done something wrong. But fear not, this chapter clues you in on what you need to know to get started with compressors. After that, only experience (and studying more advanced manuals) will make you a pro.

Understanding Audio Waveforms

Compressors are one of the hardest mixing tools for most people to understand. One reason is that, in spite of their importance, their effect is often subtle—at least it is when a compressor is used correctly. In fact, although a compressor is an audio effect, it's one you should never hear, except in comparison with the uncompressed track.

Another thing that makes compressors so hard to understand is all the esoteric controls, including stuff like threshold, ratio, attack, and release. Some compressors even include a setting called knee, although we won't be going that far in our explorations. You should already have some idea of what a compressor does from our discussions in Chapter 11. But we dig in a lot deeper now.

To truly understand compression, it helps to *see* what it does, rather than just *hear* it. So turn your attention to Figure 14.1, which shows the sound wave for "Pro Tools Blues," as we left it in the previous chapter. (Actually, the waveform is only the left channel of the stereo file.)

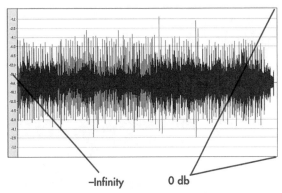

Figure 14.1   A song's wave form.

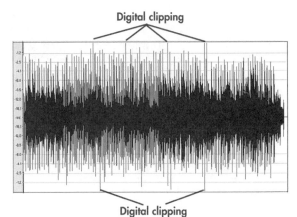

Figure 14.2   The waveform increased in level by 3 dB.

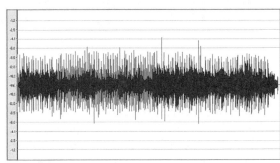

Figure 14.3   The waveform decreased in level by 3 dB.

Look at the scale on the left side of the waveform. The numbers are probably too small to see, but just know that the horizontal center-line represents a level of –infinity decibels, which you can think of as digital silence. The top and bottom of the graph represents 0 dB, which, ironically, is the highest level before *digital clipping*—a nasty form of distortion—occurs. To put it simply (you're welcome), nothing in the waveform can ever go beyond 0 dB on the graph.

Why are there two 0 dBs? And why, now that you think about it, are there two of every dB value except –infinity? Sound waves, like AC electrical current, constantly cycle up and down across their center point. Although this isn't an entirely accurate comparison, imagine that the waveform above the –infinity mark is standing on a mirror, and the stuff below the –infinity mark is the reflection.

The taller the waveform is in the graph, the higher its level, which you can inaccurately, but close enough, think of as volume. For example, if you were to increase the volume of the wave-form in Figure 14.1 by 3 dB, you'd get the wave-form shown in Figure 14.2. Conversely, if you were to decrease the volume of the waveform in Figure 14.1 by 3 dB, you'd get the waveform shown in Figure 14.3. Unfortunately, in the case of increasing the level, there wasn't enough room for the waveform's peaks to increase by 3 dB, so we now have some digital clipping in Figure 14.2.

So now you get all this waveform-level stuff, right? If not, reread the previous section until you do. You can't understand compressors visu-ally without understanding the graphs of wave-form levels.

Limiting: The Easy One

You may recall (heaven knows I've said it often enough) that a limiter is nothing more than a compressor with the pedal to the metal. Because a limiter stops a waveform's level from ever get-ting beyond a specific point, it theoretically needs only one control: *threshold*. Threshold is the point at which the limiter starts working. You can think of this as a ceiling, the highest the level can go. Figure 14.4 shows our wave-form after it has been run through a limiter with a threshold of –8.5 dB. Now, no part of the waveform exceeds –8.5 dB.

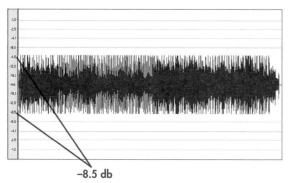

–8.5 db

Figure 14.4 The waveform limited to –8.5 dB.

I said that a limiter theoretically needs only one control. In the real world, however, a limiter often also has *attack* and *release*. Attack is how fast the limiter jumps in once the level crosses the threshold. If the attack is more than 0, some peaks may slip past the limiter, as shown in Figure 14.5. (The figure points out only a few of the peaks.) Release is how long it takes for the limiter to stop limiting once it's been activated. We'll get to release when we talk about compression.

Peaks not caught by the limiter

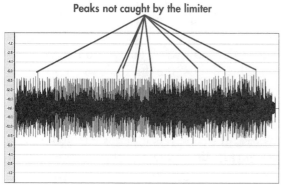

Figure 14.5 An attack greater than 0 allows some fast peaks to slip past the limiter.

One very popular use for limiting is to squish down a recording's peaks so much that you can significantly increase the overall volume. For example, Figure 14.6 shows "Pro Tools Blues" after it was limited to –10 dB and the entire level of the song increased by 10 dB. Note that the levels that reach all the way to 0 dB do not indicate digital clipping, because, thanks to the limiting, none of the peaks try to go beyond 0 dB.

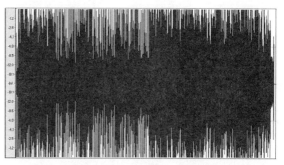

Figure 14.6 Limiting followed by a volume increase.

If you think "Pro Tools Blues" looks ridiculously squished, you should see some of the stuff from the CDs you buy every day. Heavy-metal bands especially like to squish their music down, for better or for worse, into a wall of sound. Figure 14.7, for example, shows the waveform for Dream Theater's song "Misunderstood," from the album *Six Degrees of Inner Turbulence.* As you can see from the waveform, the first part of the song is on the quiet side; when the band revs it up, however, the waveform is squished like a bug under a boot in order to get the highest possible volume onto the CD.

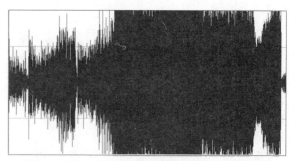

Figure 14.7 Heavy-metal groups love to squish their music flat.

Notes from the Track Sheet

Most professional engineers and producers hate to see music squished down to make the volume louder. This is because the more you squish the music with a limiter or compressor, the more dynamics you lose. Dynamics are an important part of music, and when you compress things too much, it starts to sound lifeless and bland. Still, recording artists want their CDs to be as loud as possible these days. Compression or limiting followed by a level increase is how it's done.

Compression: The Hard One

As you now know, a limiter takes a waveform level that goes beyond the threshold and shoves it back down to the threshold. A compressor, on the other hand, takes a waveform level that goes beyond the threshold and shoves it only partly back down to the threshold. This allows a waveform to retain some of its dynamic character. The waveform can still vary in level, just not as much.

The Effects of Compression

Let's take "Pro Tools Blues" again. We'll compress it with the same settings we used with the limiter back in Figure 14.4, except in this case, we'll set the compressor's ratio to 2:1. Figure 14.8 shows the results.

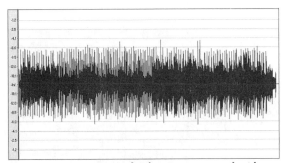

Figure 14.8 "Pro Tools Blues" compressed with a threshold of –8.5 dB, a ratio of 2:1, an attack of 1 millisecond, and a release of 500 milliseconds.

The ratio of 2:1 means that, rather than pushing peaks all the way back to the threshold, the compressor only pushes them halfway back. In more technical terms, for every 2 dB that the level goes beyond the threshold, only 1 dB is allowed to go through the compressor. So if the signal into the compressor is 8 dB above the threshold, how much does the compressor allow through? If you said 4 dB, you understand.

Notes from the Track Sheet

A limiter is just a compressor with a ratio of infinity:1. Sometimes a limiter shows a ratio of something like 100:1, which is close enough to infinity:1 for most purposes. In other words, no matter how much the waveform's level goes over the threshold, only the level represented by the threshold can come out of the limiter. In fact, many engineers consider any ratio above 10:1 to be limiting.

Dealing with Attack

Compressors have a setting called attack, which specifies how quickly the compressor starts working when the input level crosses the threshold. Suppose, for example, you have the threshold set to –8 dB and the attack set to 50 milliseconds (ms). Now, the drummer smacks his snare good and hard, and the level going into the compressor jumps up past the threshold of –8 dB. What happens? The compressor sees that it's supposed to wait 50 ms before doing anything, so it just sits there twiddling its thumbs. After 50 ms pass, the compressor jumps into action bringing the level down by the ratio you set.

Why the heck would you want the compressor to wait? That's a good question, for which I have no answer. Just kidding. (Do you really think I'd put a question in the book that I couldn't answer?) By allowing a little of the peak to get past the compression, you can keep more of the original attack of the sound. In the case of the snare drum we were just talking about, the impact of the drum stick on the drum retains its aggressiveness, making the drums sound punchier and livelier.

Back in Figure 14.8, you saw "Pro Tools Blues" compressed with a threshold of –8.5 dB, a ratio of 2:1, and an attack of 1 ms. A 1-ms attack is very fast, meaning that the compressor compresses virtually everything above the threshold. But what if you were to change the attack to 50 ms? Figure 14.9 shows the results. Now some peaks are definitely making it past the compressor.

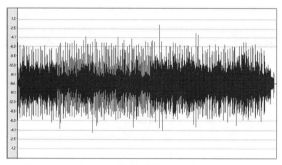

Figure 14.9 "Pro Tools Blues" compressed with a threshold of –8.5 dB, a ratio of 2:1, an attack of 50 ms, and a release of 500 ms.

Dealing with Release

Compressors also have a setting called release, which is sort of the opposite of attack. Release specifies how long the compressor keeps working once it's activated. Let's go back to our snare drum example, but now set the compressor's release time to 500 ms (half a second), while keeping the threshold and attack settings. Here's what happens:

1. The drummer hits the snare drum.

2. The level going into the compressor jumps above the threshold of –8.5 dB.

3. The compressor does nothing for 50 ms (the attack setting).

4. After 50 ms, the compressor compresses the sound level by the ratio.

5. The compressor continues to compress the signal for 500 ms (the release setting), regardless of any changing levels.

6. After 500 ms, the compressor stops working.

The next time the level goes over the threshold, this whole cycle begins again. You can see that using a compressor can be confusing. Talking about all these numbers doesn't tell you what the compressor sounds like. Unfortunately, that's just the way it is. You need to use your ears, and you need to have some experience with using tools such as compressors.

But what, you say, is the point of having a release time? Simply, it prevents the compressor from working too hard. Suppose, for example, the sound coming into the compressor is crossing the threshold every 100 ms. Without the release setting, the compressor goes on and off every tenth of a second. This causes an effect known as *pumping*.

What to Compress

The question of *how* to compress something begs the question of *what* to compress. Engineers routinely compress some tracks in a recording session, whereas others tend to go on a case-by-case basis. Obviously, anything with a dynamic range that's too great to record well needs to be compressed, and some instruments almost always fall into this category. Other instruments are routinely compressed simply because they sound better that way and fit better into a mix.

Bass Guitar

The first of these routinely compressed instruments is the bass guitar. Because it's difficult to play a bass at a constant volume, as well as because some notes invariably boom more than others, compression is usually called for. The good news is that an overly compressed bass part isn't anywhere near as noticeable as some other types of instruments might be, so you can get away with a lot of clumsiness and inexperience. But I'm not going to let that happen to you, anyway.

Vocals

The human voice is capable of a huge dynamic range, and recording it is a challenge. Engineers tend to compress vocals both when they're being recorded and when they're being mixed. Compression during recording helps keep the loud parts from distorting, whereas compression during mixing helps the vocal fit well into the mix, so that it can always be heard.

Keep in mind, however, that because the human voice is very expressive and has a lot of dynamic range, people expect to hear it that way. That is, if you overcompress a vocal, you'll take all the passion and expressiveness out of the performance. And in case you haven't figured it out, that's a bad thing.

Drums

Drums can wreak havoc in a recording session. First, you need all those freakin' microphones, and then you have to deal with a person who plays one way when you're trying to set levels, fooling you into setting your levels too high, and then plays another way when you're trying to record, blasting every track into red. Hey, it's not the drummer's fault. Drummers just get excited when the music starts.

Just as with vocals—and for the same reasons—engineers often compress drums during both recording and mixing. When recording, the compressor's task is to make sure the levels don't get too high. Limiters, too, often take on the task of taming drummers. During mixing, compressors help the drums sit nicely in the song.

Professional engineers can do a lot with compressors to make drums sound really good, enhancing the attack and adding sustain, providing more resonance. This usage is advanced stuff, though. Our goal in this book is just to learn to use compression well enough to smooth out the level of tracks in a mix.

What Not to Compress ...

… well, obviously anything that has limited dynamic range. A good example is distorted electric guitar, because the process of distortion already involves heavy compression. It doesn't matter how hard that heavy-metal guitarist hammers his strings. That guitar just ain't gonna get any louder—at least, not without turning up the amp's volume control. Compare this to that drummer whose volume is constrained only by his strength.

If you compress something that needs no compression, all you do is reduce its volume. Take a look at Figure 14.10, which shows the typically overcompressed song from a CD. See the way everything is squished up to 0 dB? No dynamic range there. Any range was long ago removed by the mastering engineer.

Figure 14.10 An overly compressed track from a CD.

Now let's take that track and compress it with a threshold of –8 dB, a ratio of 3:1, an attack of 0 ms (just to make sure we catch everything), and a release of 500 ms. Figure 14.11

shows the results. You can see that it looks exactly the same—all squished flat—except for being lower in level. Case closed.

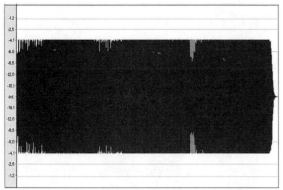

Figure 14.11   A overly compressed track that's been recompressed.

Squashing "Pro Tools Blues"

Got the blues yet? (Sorry about that.) Yep, it's time to tackle our burgeoning recording, "Pro Tools Blues." We're going to throw some compression on the bass line and the vocals. (What vocals? You'll see.) The drums don't need compressing because they were recorded from a drum machine, whose drum samples have already been processed in a pro studio. The rhythm guitar already sits well in the mix, so it'll be okay as is. The lead guitar is distorted, which, as you recall, means it's already been heavily compressed. No point in doing it again.

To get started, load up the last version of "Pro Tools Blues," which should be in your Chapter13\ProToolsBlues13 folder. This is the one that's been EQ'ed, remember? The next step is to add a compressor plug-in to the track with which you want to work—in this case, the bass guitar.

Click one of the insert buttons on the bass guitar track, but not the one assigned to the EQ. We want to leave that insert where it is. Choose the Plug-In command, and select the Compressor plug-in, as shown in Figure 14.12.

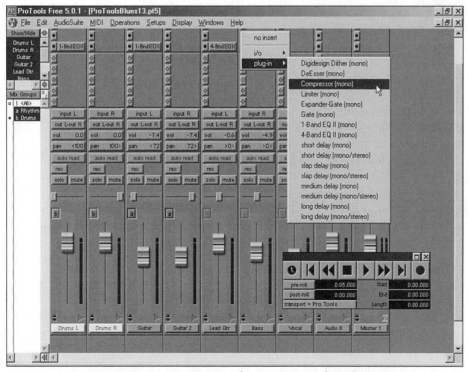

Figure 14.12   Inserting the Compressor plug-in.

When you insert the compressor, it'll appear on the screen. Set the threshold to 0 (all the way to the right), the ratio to 1.25:1 (all the way to the left), the attack to around 1.0 ms, and the release to about 500 ms. The compressor is now set to do nothing at all (Figure 14.13), as you can tell by the diagonal line in the little graph window to the right of the controls. That diagonal line means that what goes into the compressor comes out unchanged.

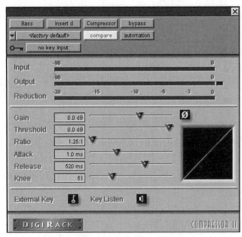

Figure 14.13   The Pro Tools Free compressor.

Click the Play button in the Transport window to play the song. Watch the Input, Output, and Reduction readouts at the top of the plug-in. The Input readout shows the level of audio coming into the compressor, and the Output readout shows the level of audio leaving the compressor. With no compression going on, both lines should show the same level. The Reduction readout shows how much the compressor is reducing the level of the audio. Nothing should be happening there.

Now set the ratio to about 4.00:1. Got it? Next, start moving the threshold control slowly to the left. Eventually, you'll start to see the Reduction readout come alive. This means that you've lowered the threshold to the point where portions of the audio are crossing the threshold and activating the compressor. Adjust the threshold until the Reduction line stays

busy but doesn't go much past –3 dB, as shown in Figure 14.14.

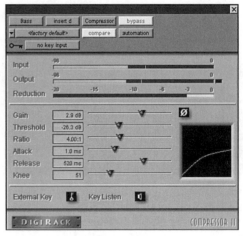

Figure 14.14   Adjusting to a max reduction of about –3 dB.

Notice the way the Reduction line keeps jumping around? This is because not all notes of the bass line require the same amount of compression. The quieter notes get almost no compression at all, while the louder ones get reduced by about 3 dB, with other notes falling somewhere in between.

Notice also that the Output readout shows less level than the Input readout. This is because the compression has lowered the average volume of the track a little. You can make up for this by increasing the gain control until Input and Output both match again. Engineers often refer to a compressor's gain control as "make-up gain."

Now, I'm finally going to have you ask a question that I can't answer. Why does the threshold of this plug-in have to be set so low before the compressor kicks in? I don't know. I'm sure I'm missing something in the 1000 pages of Pro Tools documentation, in spite of the fact that I tried to memorize every word, but I just don't know. In the case of our bass line, a threshold of –10 dB should be plenty. With the Pro Tools compressor, I ended up with a threshold of about –27 dB, which is *way* down there. Just to make sure I wasn't crazy, I replaced the Pro

Tools compressor with one from the Waves collection, and, sure enough, a threshold of –10 dB did the trick just fine. I'm sure I'm revealing some ignorance on my part, but I just couldn't let you sit there and wonder what was going on. Take some comfort in the fact that I don't know either.

Anyway, at this point, you've got a nicely compressed bass line. The next step is to do the vocals. Yeah, I know, what vocals? This is the part of the show where you scrap all the work you just did on ProToolsBlues13 and load up ProToolsBlues14, which you'll find in the Chapter14\ProToolsBlues14 folder of this book's CD.

The Chapter 14 version of "Pro Tools Blues" features a new track, which you probably already suspect is the vocals. Placing a compressor on the vocal track isn't much different from what you already did with the bass track, so I won't make you do it. It's all set for you. The thing to keep in mind about vocal compression is that you want the vocal to retain as much of its dynamic range as possible, while at the same time always being audible, but never too loud. Yep, it's a lot like balancing on a tightrope. Wear a helmet. Knee pads might not be a bad idea either.

Notes from the Track Sheet

Okay, sure the lyrics for "Pro Tools Blues" are pretty goofy. They're supposed to be. But trust me that when you start using a lot of audio software, you'll be singing the same blues! I should also mention that the lyrics in no way reflect on the quality of Pro Tools, which is one darn fine product. I'm just singing about audio software in general. The song is called "Pro Tools Blues" because it was created on Pro Tools.

I suggest that, after loading up "Pro Tools Blues," you display the compressor for the vocal track (just click the compressor's button in the inserts), and then click the compressor's

Bypass button to turn it off. Now, listen to the song with the uncompressed vocals. Take note of where the vocal seems too quiet and where it seems too loud. (I was careful to create a vocal track that went all the way from a whisper to a yell.) Then, listen to the song again with the compressor on (click the Bypass button again). Hear the difference?

Before we move on to the next chapter, eyeball the following two important rules for compression:

1. As you lower the threshold, more of your audio is compressed.
2. As you raise the ratio, the harder the audio is getting compressed.

Remember these rules forever.

The Least You Need to Know

- A limiter stops the audio level from ever getting beyond a specific point, called the threshold.
- A compressor takes the audio level that goes beyond the threshold and reduces the level by a percentage.
- A compressor's ratio specifies the output level for any given input level. For example, a ratio of 4:1 means that for every 4 dB that the level goes beyond the threshold, only 1 dB is allowed make it through the compressor.
- A compressor's attack time is how quickly the compressor starts working when the input level crosses the threshold. On the other hand, a compressor's release time is how long the compressor keeps working once it's activated.
- As you lower the threshold, more of your audio is being compressed.
- As you raise the ratio, the audio is getting more and more heavily compressed.

In This Chapter

◆ Understanding auxiliary sends

◆ Learning about inserted, postfader, and prefader effects

◆ Assigning effects to buses

◆ Controlling reverb and delay

Chapter 15

Adding Effects

All you have to do now is add a couple of effects to "Pro Tools Blues," and it'll be finished. Using effects means understanding about auxiliary sends and auxiliary tracks, topics that sound scarier than they really are. After this chapter, you'll have all this aux stuff down pat. In this chapter, you also learn how to create delayed copies of tracks without actually having to create a physical copy of the track (as you did previously with the rhythm guitar in "Pro Tools Blues"), as well as how to use reverb properly, a skill that can make the difference between a professional-sounding mix and a cheesy, amateur one.

Sends and Effects

If you're a guitarist or some other sort of musician who typically uses stomp boxes to add effects to your sound, you might think that you already have this effects stuff figured out. If so, you're in for a surprise. Sticking a box in-line with your instrument is only one way to get effects. A typical studio—including a home studio—offers three general ways to add effects:

◆ Inserting effects in-line with audio
◆ Routing audio postfader to effects
◆ Routing audio prefader to effects

The first choice in this list is the one that's most similar to the effects method used by performing musicians. Figure 15.1 shows how this works in the studio. In the figure, the audio from a vocal track goes to an effects unit, and then the output of the effects unit goes back to the track and through the fader. The fader then controls the level of the vocal/effect mix.

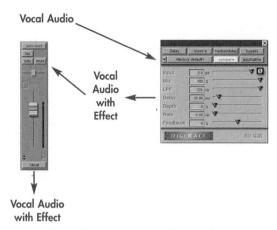

Figure 15.1   Inserting effects in-line.

This method of using effects gives you effects mixed in with the audio. We used this method when we plugged EQs and compressors into some of the tracks of the "Pro Tools Blues" session. A downside of using effects this way is that the effect can be used on only one channel at a time. For example, in the "Pro Tools Blues" case, we had to use an additional EQ plug-in for each track we EQ'ed.

During the mixing process, engineers often add effects to tracks by routing a copy of the track's audio to an external effects box or to a software plug-in. This is what happens with the remaining two methods in the previous list. The process is fairly simple, but can be confusing until you get used to it. Figure 15.2 illustrates the typical scenario, which is the postfader version.

Here, the audio takes two different paths. The first is the normal one, straight through the channel unchanged. The second path is from after the fader (postfader) to the effects unit. The output of the channel and the effects unit are then mixed together for the final audio.

Because the audio copy comes after the channel's fader, the fader controls the level of input to the effects unit. For example, when you lower the fader, you lower the level of audio going to the effect, which in turn causes

the effects unit to generate less of the effect. Simply, the fader controls the level of the audio/effects mix.

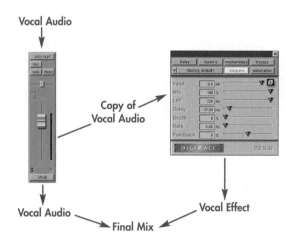

Figure 15.2   Postfader effects send.

Another way to route the audio to an effects unit is *prefader*. This means the audio copy comes from before the channel's fader and so remains at a constant level. Figure 15.3 illustrates this method.

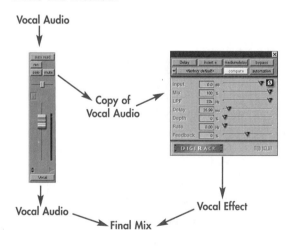

Figure 15.3   Prefader effects send.

Now, when you change the level of the track with the fader, the original audio changes, but the effect does not. If you were, for example, to lower the channel's fader, the original audio would get quieter, but the effect would stay at the same level. By the time you reduced the fader all the way, you'd have only effects.

A couple of caveats: First, the part of the mixer that sends an audio copy (appropriately called an *auxiliary send*, or, more typically, *aux send*) to an effects unit has its own level control. Moreover, the effects unit not only has level controls, it also has something called *mix*, which controls the balance between the input audio and the effect. Yikes!

The level control for an aux send is nothing more than volume for the audio copy being sent to the effects unit. You'll learn more about this when you add effects to "Pro Tools Blues." The mix control is a little more complicated, because its use changes depending on how you're using the effects unit.

Generally, when the mix control is at 0, nothing gets through the effects unit except the input audio. In other words, you'll get no effects. Conversely, when the mix control is set to 100 percent, you get nothing but effects, with none of the input audio present.

So when you're using an effects unit as an in-line insert, you'll probably want to have the mix control set to 50 percent, which causes the effects unit to output equal amounts of the input audio and the effect. Of course, if you want to add more effect, you can raise the mix control, or lower it to get less of the effect.

When you're using the effects unit in the post- or prefader configuration, you already have a "pure" copy of the track's audio coming through the track's fader, so all you want the effects unit to produce is … well … *effects*. So in these cases, the mix control is usually set to 100 percent.

> ### Notes from the Track Sheet
>
> Engineers have names for audio with or without effects. The word *dry* describes audio that contains no effects, whereas *wet* describes audio with effects. So the higher you set the mix control on an effects unit, the "wetter" the sound gets. On the other hand, lowering the mix control gives you "drier" sound.

Getting the Waves Demos

We're almost ready to do more work on "Pro Tools Blues," but first you need a reverb plug-in. Unfortunately, Pro Tools Free doesn't come with one. The good news, though, is that you can still complete this lesson without spending a lot of money, by downloading a trial version of the Waves TrueVerb.

First, go to www.waves.com, and click the Downloads link. You'll then be asked to give Waves a little information about yourself. Eventually, you'll get to the downloads page, where you should download the Waves Native Power Pack. This is a bunch of cool plug-ins, including the wonderful TrueVerb, which you'll be using to finish up "Pro Tools Blues."

Although you can't download Waves plug-in demos singly, you can buy them singly. If you want your own copy of TrueVerb—one that doesn't time out after 14 days—the price is $200.

> ### Notes from the Track Sheet
>
> Digidesign, the makers of Pro Tools, offers an inexpensive reverb plug-in for Pro Tools Free. This plug-in costs $49.95, and you can find it at secure.digidesign.com. After arriving at this web page, click the link for Pro Tools Free.

Adding Effects to "Pro Tools Blues"

Traditionally, blues songs don't use a lot of effects, instead opting for a more live sound. For that reason, we'll add only two effects to "Pro Tools Blues": reverb and delay. Before we do that, though, let's learn to make a copy of the latest "Pro Tools Blues" session. The following steps show how.

1. Load ProToolsBlues14 from the Chapter14\ProToolsBlues14 folder of this book's CD.
2. Select the File menu's Save Session Copy In command, as shown in Figure 15.4. The Save Copy of Session In dialog box appears.
3. Select the Copy Audio Files option (Figure 15.5), choose a destination folder, and then save the session under the name **ProToolsBlues15**.
4. Use the File menu's Close Session command to close the current session.

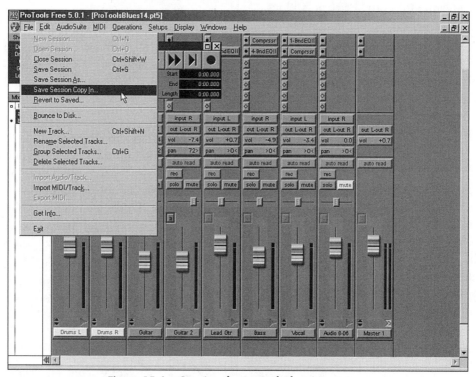

Figure 15.4   Copying the ProToolsBlues14 session.

Destination folder

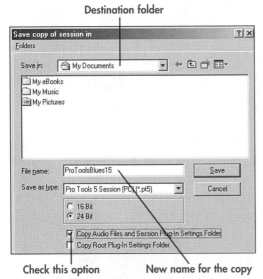

Check this option   New name for the copy

Figure 15.5   Copying the session.

Deleting Unneeded Tracks

Now that you have a copy of the session, you can experiment with adding effects without risk of changing the original session. (Of course, you always have the sessions on this book's disc.) Our first task is to create a track to host the delay effect. Using this effect, we can create a delayed rhythm guitar electronically, and so will be able to remove the delayed track we created previously. That frees up the track for other uses. We can also remove the track labeled Audio 8-06, because we've never used it for anything. Here's how to remove the two tracks:

1. In the Mix Groups window (Figure 15.6), click the Drums group to deselect it. This leaves only the Rhythm Guitar mix group selected.

Deselect the
Drums group
here

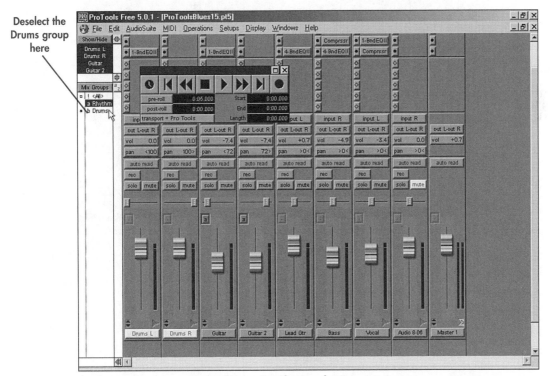

Figure 15.6   Deselecting the Drums mix group.

2. Click the Mix Groups button, and select Delete Group from the menu that appears (Figure 15.7).

3. When Pro Tools Free asks whether you're sure you want to delete the group (Figure 15.8), click the Delete button.

4. Click the Guitar 2 button to select the delayed rhythm guitar track (Figure 15.9).

5. Select the File menu's Delete Selected Tracks command (Figure 15.10).

6. When Pro Tools Free asks you if you want to delete the track, click the Delete button, as shown in Figure 15.11.

7. Delete the Audio 8-06 track using the same procedure you did to delete the Guitar 2 track.

8. Select the File menu's Save Session command to save your changes.

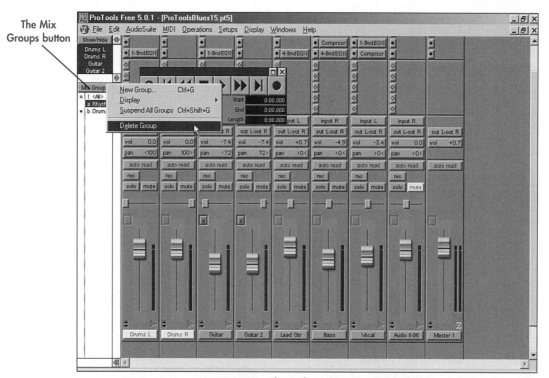

Figure 15.7   The Delete Group command.

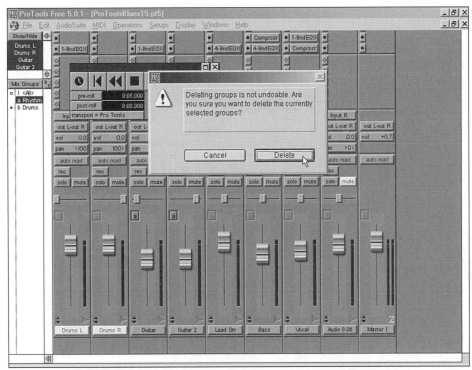

Figure 15.8   Verifying the Delete Groups command.

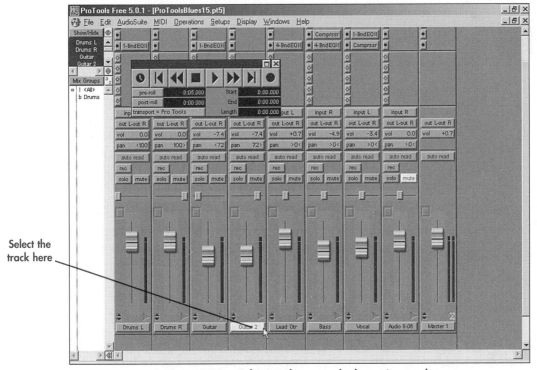

Figure 15.9   Selecting the extra rhythm guitar track.

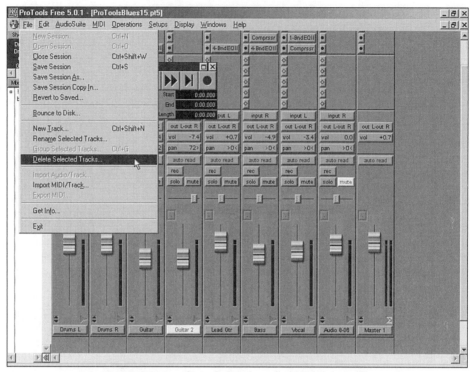

Figure 15.10   The Delete Selected Tracks command.

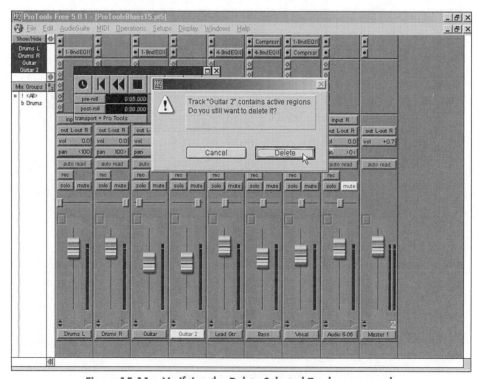

Figure 15.11   Verifying the Delete Selected Tracks command.

Adding an Auxiliary Track for the Delay Effect

Ah, it feels good to have those tracks cleaned up, doesn't it? Almost as good as taking a shower after mowing the lawn. Now we can finally get busy adding effects to the session. As I mentioned before, the first thing we'll do is add an auxiliary (aux) track for the delay effect.

What's an aux track? For our purposes, it's a special track that can receive input from one of our audio tracks. Just as important, an aux track can host effects plug-ins just like an audio track can. The cool thing is that, by using an aux track to handle the effect, we need only a

single plug-in to add the effect to any or all audio tracks in our session.

For example, we could send the audio from our guitar track to an aux track that's set up with a delay plug-in. (This is, in fact, exactly what we're going to do to replace the delayed guitar track we just deleted.) We could also send audio from other audio tracks to the same aux track to get the delay effect on them. You'll see how this works when we add reverb to the vocal and lead guitar tracks.

Follow these steps to create the delay aux track:

1. Select the File menu's New Track command (Figure 15.12).

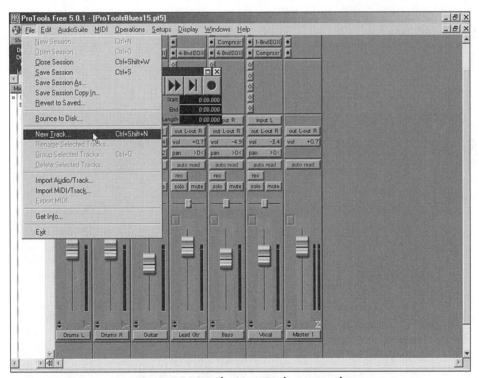

Figure 15.12   The New Track command.

2. Add an Aux Input (mono) track to the session, as shown in Figure 15.13.

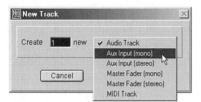

Figure 15.13 Adding a mono auxiliary-input track.

3. Double-click the new track's label (the button that reads Aux 1), and change its name to **Delay,** as shown in Figure 15.14.

4. Reposition the track so that it's between the Vocal track and the Master 1 track. To do this, drag the track's label until the vertical dotted line is positioned between the Vocal and Master 1 tracks, as shown in Figure 15.15.

5. Click the aux track's input button, as shown in Figure 15.16. A menu appears.

6. Assign the track's input to bus 1 (Figure 15.17). The track will now receive any audio that you assign to bus 1. (A bus is nothing fancier than a connection that can send audio somewhere.)

7. Raise the track's level to 0.0 (Figure 15.18).

8. Click one of the track's insert buttons, and assign the Medium Delay (mono) plug-in to the insert, as shown in Figure 15.19.

9. Set the delay's Mix control to 100 percent and the Delay control to about 35 ms, as shown in Figure 15.20. These settings mean that the effect will output only the delayed audio, with none of the input audio present. Also, the audio created by the effect will be delayed by 35 ms.

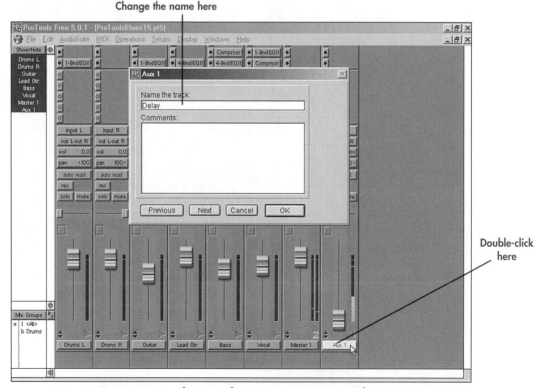

Figure 15.14 Changing the aux input's name to Delay.

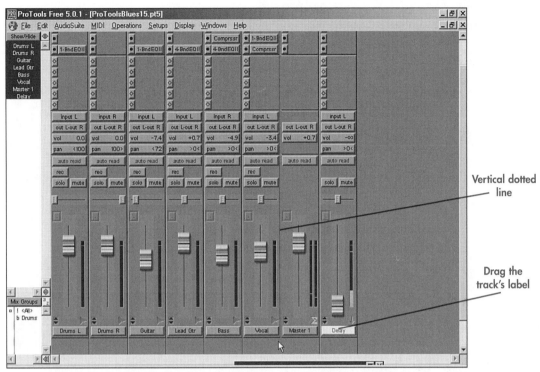

Figure 15.15   Dragging the Delay track to its new position.

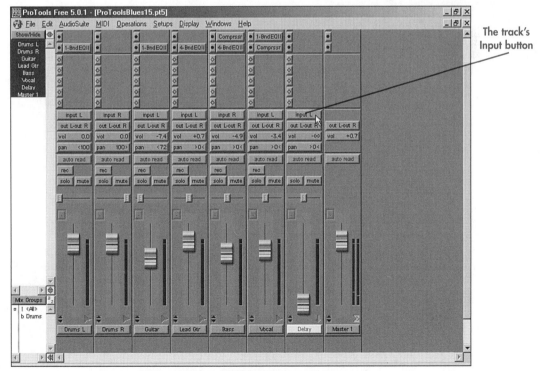

Figure 15.16   Clicking the Input button.

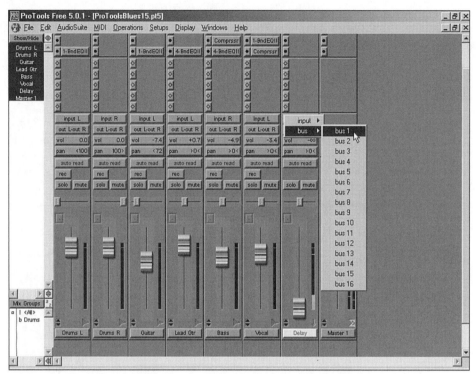

Figure 15.17   Assigning the track's input source.

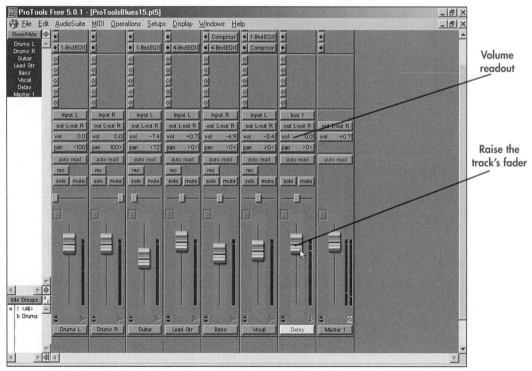

Figure 15.18   Raising the track's level.

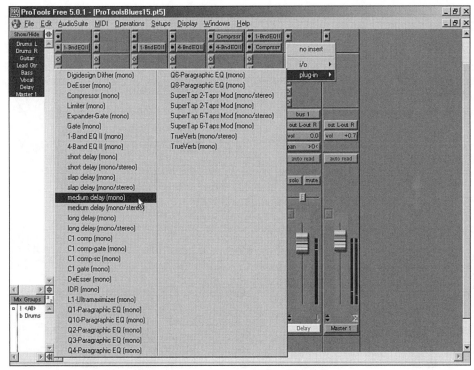

Figure 15.19 Inserting the delay effect.

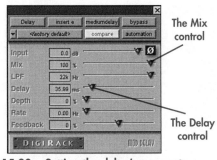

Figure 15.20 Setting the delay's parameters.

The Mix control

The Delay control

Now the aux track is all set up to provide the delay we need to double the rhythm guitar track—or any other track we want to assign to the effect. This may have seemed like a lot of work, but that's only because you had to follow the steps and learn what to do. When you get used to the process, you'll be able to set up an aux track quickly.

The delay plug-in has a lot of other settings, but we're not going to get into them here. If you want to learn more about the plug-in, you can read about it in the Pro Tools documentation that you downloaded and installed.

Assigning the Delay to the Rhythm Guitar

To create a delayed copy of the rhythm guitar track, we need to send a copy of the guitar's audio to the Delay track. It's really that simple. In fact, you only need to perform a few steps. Here they are:

1. Click one of the Guitar track's send buttons, as shown in Figure 15.21.

2. Assign the send to bus 1, as shown in Figure 15.22. The bus's settings window pops up.

3. Set the send level to 0.0 (Figure 15.23).

The send
buttons

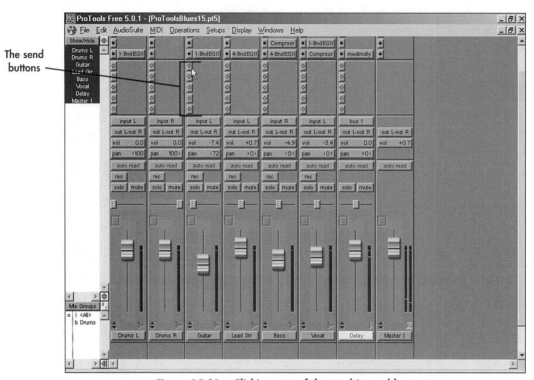

Figure 15.21 Clicking one of the track's send buttons.

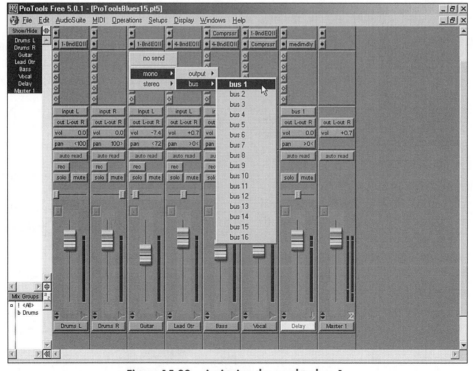

Figure 15.22 Assigning the send to bus 1.

Figure 15.23   Setting the send level.

One last thing for the delay. Because we're using it to create another guitar on the right, you need to set the Delay channel's pan control to the right. Set it to 72> (Figure 15.24), which is the exact opposite of the pan setting on the original Guitar track. The ability to pan

the effect is another advantage of having it on its own track.

Now, go ahead and listen to "Pro Tools Blues." Even though you've deleted the Guitar 2 track, you should still hear a second guitar on the right. This phantom guitar is the delayed Guitar track generated by the delay plug-in in the Delay track. Click the Delay track's Mute button to remove the effect. See? It's really coming from that channel. Would I lie? (Maybe, but not to you.)

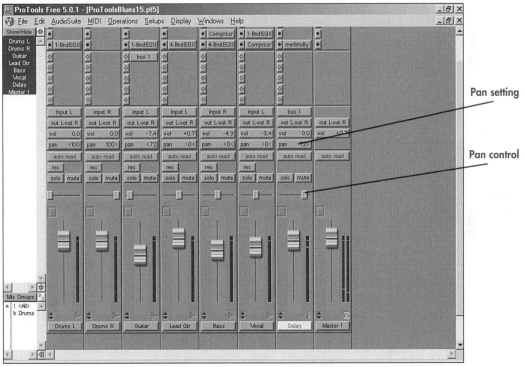

Figure 15.24   Panning the delay effect.

Adding Reverb to the Session

Okay, we've got our delay crankin'. Now let's turn our attention to the reverb. In most cases, reverb is a stereo effect, which means that we need a stereo aux track to put it on. Here's how:

1. Add an Aux Input (stereo) track to the session, as shown in Figure 15.25. If necessary, drag the track into position between Delay and Master 1.

2. Change the track's name to **Reverb** (Figure 15.26).

3. Set the track's input to bus 1-bus 2, as shown in Figure 15.27. Bus 1 carries the left side of the stereo signal, and bus 2 carries the right side.

4. Raise the level of the track to 0.0.

5. Insert the TrueVerb (stereo) plug-in into the track, as shown in Figure 15.28.

6. When the TrueVerb splash screen appears (Figure 15.29), dismiss it by clicking the X in the upper-right corner.

7. On the reverb plug-in, set the decay time to 3.0 (Figure 15.30). To do this, double-click the button and type in the value **3.0.**

8. On the reverb plug-in, set the Direct mix setting as low as it will go. To do this, double-click the button and type in the value **–24** (Figure 15.31). This removes all of the original audio from the reverb's output, leaving only the reverb.

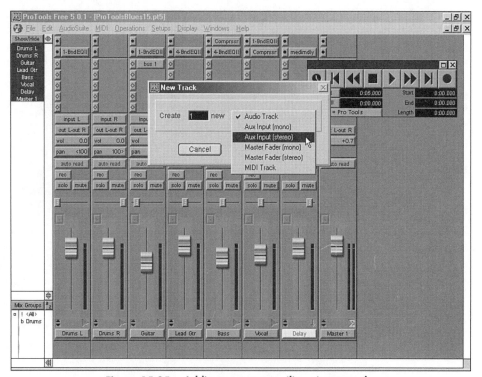

Figure 15.25   Adding a stereo auxiliary-input track.

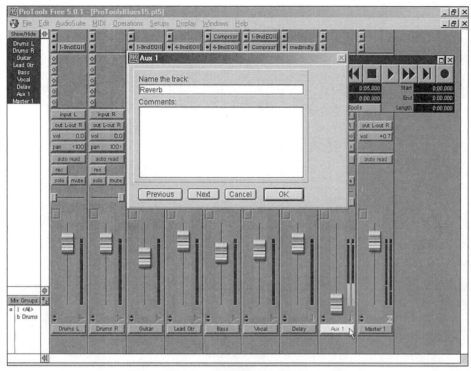

Figure 15.26   Changing the track's name.

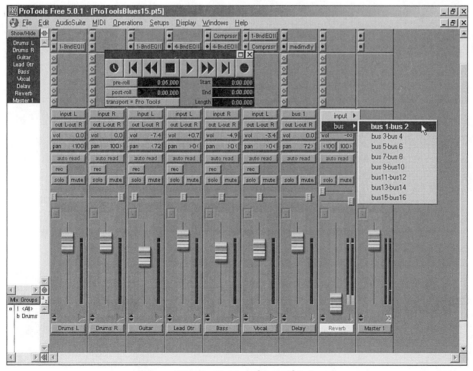

Figure 15.27   Setting the track's input.

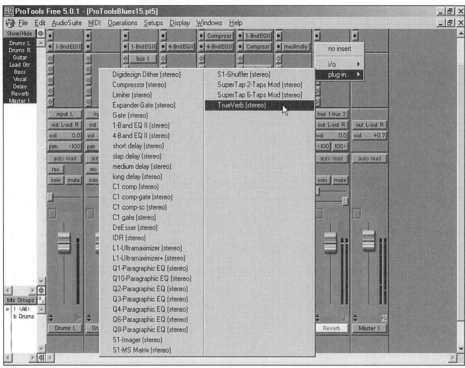

Figure 15.28   Inserting the reverb plug-in.

Figure 15.29   Dismissing the Waves splash screen.

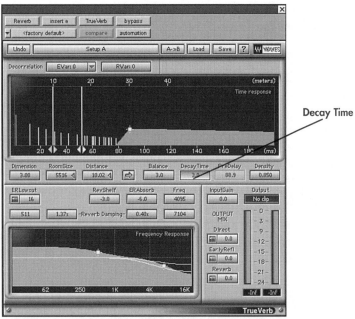

Figure 15.30   Setting the reverb's Decay Time.

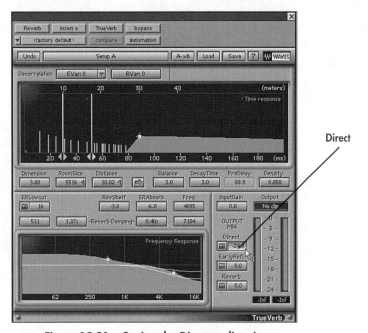

Figure 15.31   Setting the Direct audio mix.

Notes from the Track Sheet

Unless you have duct tape wrapped around your eyes, you've probably noticed that the TrueVerb plug-in has more settings than the Milky Way has stars. I could spend the next 40 pages explaining them all to you, but I've got to get this book finished sometime before I'm too decrepit to type. For our purposes in this book, it's enough for you to know that the reverb's decay time is how long it takes for the reverb effect to fade away. Please feel free to experiment with other settings, as well as to peruse the documentation that comes with the plug-in.

Vocal and Guitar Reverb

Now you've got a reverb effect that you can use with any track in the session. All you have to do is send audio from the track to bus 1-bus 2 and—*presto!*—reverb. You can control the amount of reverb for a particular track by adjusting the track's aux send volume. If this still sounds Greek to you, don't worry about it. I'll give you step-by-step instructions. In fact, here they are, all two of them:

1. Click one of the Vocal track's send buttons, and assign it to bus 1-bus 2, as shown in Figure 15.32.

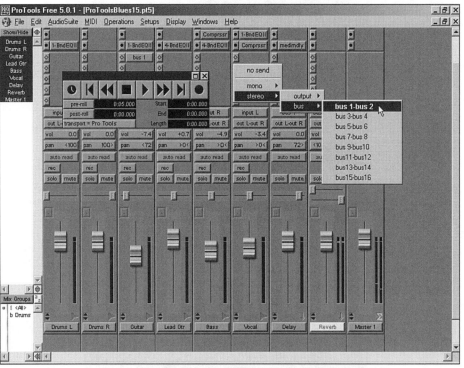

Figure 15.32 Assigning the vocal send to bus 1-bus 2.

2. Adjust the send level to about 0 (Figure 15.33).

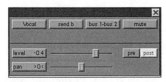

Figure 15.33   Setting the vocal send level to about 0.

When you play "Pro Tools Blues" now, you should hear reverb on the vocals. You should, in fact, hear way too much reverb. Reverb should usually be subtle. To set the reverb level correctly, click the vocal track's bus 1-bus 2 button, and when the Bus window appears, set the level to –4.8. You should also adjust the level of the vocal track with its fader, setting it to –6.4. These settings provide the right amount of reverb and level for the track.

Now, it's time to add reverb to the lead guitar track. You do this exactly as you did with the vocal track, assigning one of the lead guitar track's

sends to bus 1-bus 2. Set the send level to –4.4, and set the track's level to –1.2. You got it!

A Little Trouble

Have you noticed a little problem with the settings we're using for the buses? Bus 1 goes to the delay plug-in, right? Bus 1 and Bus 2 go to the reverb plug-in. This means that bus 1 feeds both the delay and the reverb. Because you assigned (that's right; I'm blaming you) the rhythm guitar track's send to bus 1, that track is getting both delay and reverb. The vocal and lead guitar tracks are getting a little delay, too. Ouch!

Fixing this problem is easy. We only have to assign the delay effects plug-in to a different bus. First, click the input button for the Delay track, and set it to bus 3, as shown in Figure 15.34. Now, click the send button on the Guitar track, and change it to bus 3. Make sure the send level is 0.0. All fixed!

Figure 15.34   Changing the Delay track's input to bus 3.

Notes from the Track Sheet

Normally, when you assign your buses, you would try to avoid the little overlapping problem we had with "Pro Tools Blues," where we sent one bus to two different effects tracks. In this case, though, I wanted you to see how easy it is to change the bus assignments. Of course, there's no rule that says you can't overlap buses, if that's what you want to do. I promise that the bus police won't come knocking on your door.

Effects on All-in-One Workstations

Most all-in-one workstations come with effects, although high-end units often offer them as optional upgrades. The Roland VS series of workstations, for example, offer effects on circuit boards that you purchase separately and plug into the bottom of the machine.

The Tascam 788, on the other hand, comes complete with effects, although you're limited to only two effects at a time. Still, the machine offers a wide range of effects from reverb to chorus. Moreover, you can overcome the two-effects-at-a-time problem by setting a single unit to provide multiple effects. You could, for example, have the first effects unit provide a combination of compressor, distortion, noise gate, flanger, and reverb. Similarly, the second effects unit can offer compression on up to eight channels at a time. Very cool.

Everything you learned about using effects in this chapter can be applied to all-in-one workstations. Only the mechanics are different. The Tascam 788, for example, has aux sends that route audio to the effects units. You can also choose to use insert, postfader, or prefader configurations. The 788 displays the many settings in its LCD display, and you adjust them with buttons on the console.

Where Do We Go from Here?

And that's about all we have time for. You should now have the skills to record and mix your own music at home. This isn't to say that you don't have a trainload more to learn. We've only covered the basics in this book. Your task now is to study, study, study. First, make sure you know everything in this book, and then study the Pro Tools documentation. Also study the documentation for any plug-ins you have.

Your local bookstore should have plenty of more advanced books on the topic of recording studios. The Internet, too, is a wonderful source of helpful information. Just type **home recording** into your favorite search engine. Several great magazines, too, dedicate content to recording. These include *Electronic Musician*, *Recording*, *Home Recording*, and *Mix* (although *Mix* targets professionals rather than hobbyists).

Before long, I expect to see your name in the *Billboard* top 100. Until then, don't let the reverb bite ya!

The Least You Need to Know

◆ When inserting an effect in-line, the audio goes from a track to the effect, and then the output of the effect goes back to the track and through the fader.

◆ In the postfader configuration, the audio takes two different paths. The first is straight through the channel and the second is from after the channel's fader to the effects unit. The output of the channel and the effects unit are then mixed together for the final audio.

◆ In the prefader configuration, the audio copy comes before the channel's fader and so remains at a constant level.

◆ Audio going to an effect travels via an aux send assigned to a bus.

◆ An effects unit receives audio from an aux input assigned to a bus.

◆ The mix control on an effect specifies the balance between the "dry" sound and the effects.

Appendix A

Glossary

ADAT   A format of digital tape recording, utilizing Super VHS tape, developed by Alesis.

ADAT light pipe   This connector enables you to send eight audio channels across a tiny optical cable.

attack   How fast a limiter or compressor jumps in once the level crosses the threshold.

bandwidth   A group of audio frequencies comprised of a center frequency and surrounding frequencies.

bidirectional   A microphone response pattern that picks up sound from the front and rear, but not from the sides. Also known as figure eight.

bus   An electronic path that carries audio from one place to another in a mixer.

cardioid   A microphone response pattern that picks up sound from the from mostly in front. Also called unidirectional.

chorus   An effect that works by creating delays between copies of a sound, making the original sound big and sumptuous.

compression   A compressor automatically reduces the level of sound when it gets too loud. Unlike a limiter, however, a compressor doesn't have an absolute limit on the level. Instead, a compressor reduces the level of overly loud sounds by a percentage.

condenser microphones   Among the best and most expensive microphones you can buy. They tend to be much more sensitive to high frequencies than dynamic microphones. However, they are also more sensitive to sudden loud sounds. Condenser microphones also require a power supply.

DAT   The abbreviation for digital audio tape, a digital form of cassette.

decibel   A measurement of sound intensity. Abbreviated dB.

delay   A single-repeat echo. Usually studio engineers use delay to "double" a sound, but it can also be used to repeat a sound multiple times.

digital clipping   The type of distortion caused when a digital audio signal's volume goes higher than 0 dB.

drum loops   Professionally recorded drum parts that you can string together in various ways to construct a drum track for a song.

drum machine   An electronic device that plays drum parts for your songs.

dry   Describes audio that contains no effects.

dynamic effect   Controls the dynamic range of audio. Compressors and limiters are dynamic effects.

dynamic microphones   Dynamic microphones are cheaper and sturdier than condenser mics and can take a lot of sound pressure from loud instruments. They tend, however, not to respond as well to high frequencies. Dynamic microphones require no external power.

echo   Distinct repetitions of the original sound.

EQ   Short for equalization, which is used to adjust the frequency content of audio.

faders   The volume controls on each channel of a mixer.

flanging   Related to delay in that it's a time-based effect. Rather than having a single delay time, however, a flanger varies the length of time between delayed copies of the original sound and combines them to create a constantly changing filter.

flat frequency response   All audible frequencies reproduced at the same level.

graphic EQ   A type of equalizer that uses dozens of sliders to modify frequency content, creating a kind of picture of the resultant sound.

high-pass filter   Enables only high-frequency content to pass through.

high-shelf EQ   Boosts or cuts all frequencies above a specific frequency.

hypercardioid   A special form of the cardioid microphone response pattern.

impedance   A measure of resistance for alternating current. There are both low-impedance (low-Z) and high-impedance (high-Z) microphones, and they are not interchangeable.

insert   A special type of jack that handles both input and output to and from a device.

latency   The delay caused by the time it takes for audio software to process sound.

limiter   A device that allows sound levels to get to a maximum point, after which the sound cannot get any louder

line-matching transformer   An adapter that enables you to plug a low-impedance device into a high-impedance input and vice versa.

low-pass filter   Enables only low-frequency content to pass through.

low-shelf EQ   Boosts or cuts all frequencies below a specific frequency.

mastering   Giving the songs you've recorded the final polish they need before they're recorded onto a CD or some other recording medium.

MIDI   Stands for Musical Instrument Digital Interface and is a standardized way of controlling electronic musical instruments through a set of predefined commands.

mixing   The process of converting a multitrack recording to the stereo (or sometimes surround sound) format.

monitor   A studio speaker.

multitrack recorder   A special type of recorder that enables a musician to record many instruments onto separate tracks.

near-field monitors Studio speakers that are designed to be placed close to the mixing console. This is the type of speaker used in most home studios.

omnidirectional A microphone response pattern that picks up sound from everywhere.

overdubbing Recording new tracks that are added to a set of previously recorded tracks.

panning Positioning sounds within the stereo spectrum.

parametric EQ A type of equalizer that can manipulate only a few frequencies at a time. This is the type of EQ often built in to mixers.

phase shifting An effect caused by constantly changing the phase relationship between the original sound and copies of the sound.

plug-ins Software modules that can be added to a host program such as Pro Tools.

postfader Acquiring a source sound from after the fader. The fader then controls the level of the output.

powered speakers Studio monitors that have built-in amplifiers.

punching-in Rerecording a small part of a performance by turning the record function on and off as the musician plays.

Q The bandwidth affected by an equalizer.

ratio The amount by which a compressor reduces audio that surpasses the threshold.

release How long it takes for a limiter or compressor to stop processing once it's been activated.

reverb An effect that mimics the echoey interior of various sized rooms.

signal processors Devices, such as effects units, that modify audio in some way.

stereo image The position of various sounds in a stereo mix.

stereo separation How well the left and right channels of a stereo program are isolated from each other.

supercardioid A special form of the cardioid microphone response pattern.

sweep control On a parametric EQ, the control that selects the frequency to manipulate.

threshold The audio level at which a limiter or compressor starts working.

virtual tracks A number of separate recordings associated with the same track. To listen back to a take, you plug it into the track.

wet Describes audio that contains effects.

An Introduction to Mastering

For most people, the art of mastering is a mystery. Most people, in fact, don't even know what mastering is. Even for musicians who have had some experience with mastering, the process remains somewhat of a black art. This is because professional-level mastering requires years of training and deals with the minutest details of a recording.

What is mastering? Generally, mastering is giving the songs you've recorded the final polish they need before they're pressed forever onto a CD or some other recording medium. Mastering also helps your music sound consistent on a wide variety of playback systems. Although you can probably handle the easier mastering tasks, others tasks require a sophisticated knowledge of sound and the tools used to manipulate it. In fact, if you're planning to sell your music, you should hire a professional mastering engineer, rather than attempt the mastering on your own.

The cost of mastering a full-length CD varies, but, if you hire a professional, you can expect to pay at least $1,000 and probably more. For some of us, the cost is prohibitive, so we just have to struggle along on our own. This appendix covers the mastering process and what you can do on your own to put the final polish on that set of songs you just recorded and mixed.

Mastering Software

Mastering on your computer requires mastering software. Pro Tools Free already includes most of what you need, including EQ and compressors. However, you might, if you've got the dough, want to invest in digital editing software that's better designed for the task.

A relatively inexpensive way to go is Sonic Foundry's Sound Forge Studio, which you can pick up for about $70. This "lite" version, however, cannot deal with 24-bit sound files. The limit is 16-bit sound files, which, for most cases, is just fine, since you'll probably be going to

CD, anyway, and even though most recording systems can handle either 16- or 24-bit recording, all CDs are 16-bit.

If you need some pocket relief from a thick wallet, you could spring for the full version of Sound Forge, which goes for about $350. Everything you could possibly need for a mastering job comes with this professional version.

Another popular audio package is Steinberg's Wavelab. Just as with Sound Forge, Wavelab comes in two versions, one for the cash challenged and one for folks with thicker wallets. The more inexpensive choice is Wavelab Essential, which goes for about $200. The full version is called Wavelab 4.0 and goes for about $450.

There are a lot of other choices, too. You might consider a quick trip to your local professional music store to get advice on what software is best for you. In any case, once you have a good audio editor, you're ready to entering the world of mastering. Which, of course, we're going to do right now …

Mastering Tasks

Mastering involves more than just one job, and is, in fact, a whole series of tasks. Some of these tasks require only limited experience, whereas other require expert knowledge of mastering tools, such as equalizers and compressors. The general mastering tasks include the following:

◆ Determining song order

◆ Setting the amount of space between songs

◆ Balancing the volume of each song

◆ EQing songs so that they sound sonically similar

◆ Compressing songs to tame dynamics

A professional can also help clean up a recording in many other ways, but that sort of sonic manipulation is beyond the scope of this book.

Determining Song Order

Deciding the song order on a final CD is a task often tackled by a producer and artist together. The idea is to present the songs such that they provide the greatest impact on the listener.

You may have noticed that most CDs start off with their strongest tracks—may, in fact, begin with the song that the producer has picked as the album's first single. The idea here is to impress the listener immediately, in the same way that a film director tries to drag you into his or her story as quickly as possible. Similarly, CDs often end with songs that leave the listener wanting more.

In between the first and last songs, you have a lot of room for experimentation. There are a few things to watch out for, though. You don't want to place similar songs too close together. This includes not only songs that may be similar in style or melody, but also in meter and key—unless, of course, that's the effect you're going for.

You'll also want to mix up songs such that the mellower songs are evenly intermixed with the upbeat numbers. This helps a group of songs sound more cohesive. Failure to consider this rule when determining song order could leave you with a CD that sounds as if it were recorded by two different groups.

Setting the Amount of Space Between Songs

On most CDs, the mastering engineer places a short silence—usually about two seconds—between each song. Unless you have a good reason for doing otherwise, you should stick with the typical two-second song gap. Music listeners are accustomed to this gap length and will be taken by surprise if you change it.

Taking the listener by surprise, though, isn't always a bad thing. Leaping from one track almost immediately into the next can be a powerful effect. The effect can also be disorienting when used incorrectly. If you want to experiment with the gaps between songs, feel free, but listen carefully to what the shorter gap does to the transitions between your songs.

You'll almost never want to make a gap between songs much longer than two seconds—not unless you're trying to bore your listener into a coma!

Balancing the Volume of Each Song

You don't want your listener reaching for the volume control from one song to the next. The volume of each song should be such that volume adjustments are unnecessary. This task can be trickier than you might think.

As discussed earlier in this book, the peaks in a song's waveform do not represent volume, or loudness, which is actually an average level over time. This means that just increasing the level of each song so that it peaks at 0 dB will not give you a volume-balanced CD. The best way to volume-balance your songs is to use your ears.

Start with the loudest song, perform any compression and EQing that you think it needs, and then use this track as your blueprint. Take the remaining songs and adjust their volume to properly match your blueprint song.

Don't forget that a volume-balanced CD is not necessarily one on which every song is exactly the same loudness. Do you really want that acoustic guitar number to be the same volume as that metal rocker? Not if you want your listener to stay away from the volume control.

EQing Songs

Chances are that all your songs do not sound the same from the point of view of frequency content. One song, for example, may sound brighter than another, whereas another may have more bass. Just as you don't want your listener reaching for the volume control, neither do you want her reaching for the tone controls.

Using a little EQ on your final mixes can help them sound more alike. Remember, however, that any EQ you apply at this point affects the entire song. That is, if you EQ the cymbals so they're not as bright, you're also going to change the sound of other instruments with high-end energy, such as the high-hat and snare drum. Even your guitars and keyboards will sound a little different.

You might guess that, when it comes to mastering and EQ, turning to a professional is the best bet. You can completely destroy the sound of your mixes if you don't know what you're doing. Still, fiddling a little (key word "little") with the high- and low-end can help smooth out the differences between songs.

Compressing Songs

Here's another area that's often best left to the pros, but if you insist on saving that $1,000 (who can blame you?), you can try a little compression on your own. How much depends on what you're going for.

If you want to squash your tracks down flat to attain maximum volume, you first want to run the tracks through a limiter whose threshold is set to the amount of extra volume you want. For example, if you want to add 6 dB of volume to a song, you'd first run it through a limiter with a threshold of –6 dB and an attack of 0. Then you can increase the level of the track by 6 dB, without pushing any peaks into distortion.

If all you want to do is smooth out a track's dynamics a little, you want to use a compressor set to very conservative settings. You might, for example, try a ratio of 2:1, an attack of 50 milliseconds, and a release of 500 milliseconds. Then, set the threshold so that the compressor works only on the peaks.

Just remember that compression can never be reversed. Make sure you keep copies of your tracks without compression, so you can always go back and start over. If you decide that mastering really isn't for you after all, those "virgin" tracks will come in handy when you hire a professional mastering engineer. He won't want anything to do with the results of your home mastering!

MIDI and the Recording Process

MIDI stands for Musical Instrument Digital Interface and is a standardized way of controlling musical instruments through a set of predefined commands. These commands take the place of recorded information, enabling any MIDI-capable musical instrument to reproduce a song that was previously captured via MIDI.

If this sounds a little confusing, imagine that you play a simple melody on a keyboard. Now, you want someone else to be able to play the same melody, so you write down a set of commands telling the person which keys to push and how long to hold them down. This is the idea behind MIDI. A MIDI recording doesn't contain musical information, but rather the commands needed to reproduce musical information.

MIDI is most commonly used with keyboards, but can be implemented on any electronic device that can convert information into MIDI commands. For this reason, MIDI is often used as a command language to control devices such as mixers and effects units. Many effects units, for example, respond to MIDI commands for changing the various parameters of an effect.

I don't use MIDI much in my studio. But I do have a MIDI keyboard that I use to control a hardware sound module. (Anything that controls MIDI devices is called, logically enough, a *MIDI controller*.) When I press a key on the keyboard, the keyboard sends a MIDI command to the sound module, telling it what note to play. The keyboard itself makes no sound; it only sends commands to the sound module, which makes the sound that I record on a track.

Over the years, MIDI has become much more powerful and versatile. For example, you might have a drum machine that can communicate between itself and a multitrack recorder. The recorder might send MIDI commands to the drum machine, telling it when to start and stop. This means that you don't have to waste tracks recording the drum machine. Instead, the drum machine automatically plays along with your recording.

Most multitrack recording software, including Pro Tools, can capture MIDI data as a track. Then, when you play the session back, the software sends the MIDI information to a musical instrument, most likely a keyboard or sound module, which uses the MIDI commands to reproduce the music represented by the MIDI track.

Suppose you want to record a MIDI keyboard track in your Pro Tools session. Here's the general procedure:

1. Plug the keyboard's MIDI-out into the MIDI interface connected to your computer.

2. Create a new MIDI track in Pro Tools. (This is similar to creating a new audio track.)

3. Start recording and play the keyboard. Pro Tools captures the MIDI commands coming from the keyboard and stores them in the MIDI track.

The track you've created this way contains no audio information. Instead it contains a stream of MIDI commands that can be played back into any MIDI-capable instrument. You could, for example, plug your computer's MIDI-out into a MIDI-capable sound module. Then, when you played the session back, Pro Tools sends the MIDI commands out to the sound module, which uses the commands to reproduce the part that you played on the keyboard.

Because the MIDI information contains only commands, you can use your recorded MIDI track to trigger any kind of sound you want. For example, maybe you've got your sound module or MIDI keyboard set up for an electric piano sound. When you play back the MIDI track, you get electric piano. With a quick twist of a dial, you change your sound module to a trumpet sample. Now when you play back the MIDI track, you get trumpets instead of piano.

The process isn't quite as simple as I've just described it. One complication is that MIDI commands can be transmitted on one of 16 different channels, which enable 16 different MIDI instruments to play simultaneously.

Also, MIDI supports a ton more commands than note and note duration. MIDI commands also include information on how hard a key was struck (velocity), controller data (such as vibrato), sound patch changes (when you want to switch, say, from piano to organ), and much more. In fact, some manufacturers of MIDI devices also create their own unique MIDI commands, called system exclusive data, that control their devices.

A full discussion of MIDI is beyond the scope of this book, which is dedicated to recording and mixing audio tracks. You might, however, want to explore the MIDI capabilities built in to Pro Tools. MIDI provides a powerful way to store, edit, and reproduce music, as well as to control different types of devices.

Improve Your Drum Programming by Dan Palladino

For nondrummers, coming up with realistic-sounding drum parts can be an intimidating prospect. After all, drummers study and practice for years to be able to play solid time, mark phrases, and interact with other musicians. But even if you can't keep very good time or play the lick to "Wipeout," you can still capture the essence of what drummers do by using your most important instrument—your ears.

By doing some simple transcribing and concentrating on one drum at a time, you can create some convincing parts. First, let's talk about some very basic drum-recording guidelines:

1. Make sure the kick and snare are panned near the center. (I like to pan the bass and kick drum slightly off-center to opposite sides, so they don't get in each other's way.) If your recording gets knocked down to mono, or is played back on a mono device, the kick and snare will be completely lost unless they are near the center.

2. I prefer to have the hi-hat a hair off-center to the left. (I mix drums from the drummer's perspective. Some folks like to hear it from the audience's perspective—if that's you, your hi-hat would be slightly to the right.)

3. Everything else is a matter of preference. I like to pan the other cymbals a little farther to each side. Sometimes it's cool to have the toms spread out across the stereo spectrum a la Neil Peart. If I'm using percussion, I pan those instruments hard left and right, so that each sound has its own little space in the mix. On certain types of music, it may be more appropriate to not stray too far from the center position, sounding almost mono.

Remember, when you are standing in front of a drum kit, you hear everything coming from a single source—very close to mono.

Now let's do some transcribing. Find a song with a simple beat. Aerosmith's "Walk This Way" is a good place to start. Transcribing requires careful listening and breaking down parts into their basic elements. Let's just concentrate on the kick and snare for now. Sing it: boom bap, ba-boom boom bap. Boom bap, ba-boom boom bap. Hey, you're transcribing!

Now let's listen to the straight eighth note hi-hat part. Sing it to yourself—don't forget the open hat that occurs on beat one of every bar. By breaking the beat down into two basic elements, we're now able to record it one piece at a time.

I've found that the most realistic parts are created using some type of pad setup. This way you can whack away like a real drummer using sticks. If drum pads are not available to you, a keyboard or those little tiny pads on a drum machine will do.

Record the kick and snare on one pass, and then go back and record the hi-hat separately. If you can help it, don't quantize every part you record. Quantization makes everything a little too perfect, making your parts sound machine-like. Use it sparingly. If you want to make sure the snare hits squarely on beats two and four, go ahead and quantize it. However, you will have a more realistic sound if you can leave the hi-hat unquantized. This will let the hi-hat part breathe a little bit.

Don't forget—a drummer pushes and pulls the time from section to section. For instance, it's not uncommon to push the tempo a little when making the transition from verse to chorus. Don't be afraid to push the tempo going into the chorus, and leave it at the quicker tempo. All musicians play behind, on top of,

and ahead of the beat when it's called for. Experiment with that concept in your drum parts—you add human feel that way.

Learning to break drum parts down in this way gives you a great advantage. If you start with simple beats and work your way up to more complex ones, you will have the playing of every great drummer at your disposal.

Are you writing a tune that needs a funky kind of groove to really make it work? Get a copy of *James Brown's 25 Greatest Hits* and go shopping for drum grooves. Once you find one that would work well with your song, break it down into its kick-snare and hi-hat elements, and you're on your way.

Are you working on a rap/metal kind of thing? Grab a Limp Bizkit CD and do a little transcribing.

Now some of you may be thinking that working this way is cheating. If you are under the age of 26, you probably don't know why anyone would object to this approach—you came up in the age of sampling, so borrowing tracks and turning them around for your own use isn't such a foreign idea to you. In fact, there are tons of programs out there that allow you to sample and create drum loops very easily. I'm not advocating the thievery of others' work by any means. All we're doing here is taking a basic foundation and applying it to different music. Your song is going to sound like you no matter what drumbeats are on it, and you'll find the need to modify the original beats to fit the music you're writing anyway.

To learn any new skill, we must first copy from others. With experience comes the ability to find your own unique voice. After a while, you won't need to listen to CDs to come up with beats—they'll come out of you naturally. Until that day comes, however, you will need to copy. Don't feel bad about it—everyone does it. It's just that nobody wants to admit to it.

Happy transcribing!

Case Studies

The best way to learn about recording is to do it, of course. The next best way is to listen to other recordings and discover how they were created. In this appendix, you get a chance to read about a few songs that have been placed on this book's disc for your study as well as—I hope—your listening pleasure.

Although I would have loved to provide case studies of some classic recordings, copyright laws prevent that without big royalty fees (not to mention having to track down the engineers and producers involved and get them to write descriptions of their work). With that in mind, you'll have to be happy with three songs of mine, as well as two additional tracks by a great indie group named Mung Brothers.

Here's how to proceed:

1. Listen to the song in question (you can find them all in the Case Studies folder on this book's CD).
2. Read the song's case history.
3. Listen to the song again, paying special attention to the information provided in the case history.

Please note that all the case study songs are copyrighted by their respective artists and are provided here for the sole purpose of these case studies. For more information on my music, please go to www.mp3.com/ClayWalnum. Similarly, for more information on the Mung Brothers' music, go to www.mp3.com/MungBrothers.

Case Study #1

"She's Tall Enough (For Me)"
by Clay Walnum
© 1998 by Clayton Walnum
Case study by Clayton Walnum

I recorded this song quite a while ago, and in listening to it today, there's a lot I don't like about it. First, the playing is a little sloppy in places, especially the bass guitar. Second, the drums were recorded from a drum machine, so they don't sound particularly authentic, although I did overdub a real hi-hat. Finally, the recording in general could be a lot better. This song was basically a demo that kept growing with production tricks.

You can hear some of those tricks in the song's introduction, by which I mean all that stuff that starts with the synthesizer and goes until the actual song begins. This song was recorded on an Alesis ADAT digital eight-track recorder using a Mackie 24×4 mixer. By the time I had all the basic tracks recorded, I had all eight tracks filled on the ADAT. At this point, the song had no introduction except for a few extra measures of the main riff at the start of the song. I wanted to do something cool but was out of tracks, so I either had to bounce down (premix) the main tracks to stereo, which would free up six more tracks at the expense of my never being able to redo the main mix; do all the cool stuff "live"; or do it manually as the ADAT played back the main mix.

I chose the manual route. First, I took all the vocals from the song's bridge and mixed them to a DAT (Digital Audio Tape; the digital version of a cassette). Then, I set up my Roland JP-8000 synthesizer to play the repeating pattern you hear at the start of the intro. Finally, I set up the final mix to record to my computer through an Echo Layla interface.

To put the parts all together, I started the computer to record the final mix, then started the ADAT, which played back the song's main tracks. However, the level of the mixer's main output was pulled all the way down, so the song couldn't yet be heard. With the two recorders going, I started the synthesizer, which played the synth part on its own. (All I had to do was touch a key to get the synth started, after which I could ignore it.) As the synth played, I faded the vocal part in and out, soaking it with tons of reverb to give it a far-away sound. Next, I faded the main song, also soaked in reverb on the ADAT in and out of the mix. Finally, I faded the main song in, without the reverb.

Yep, I had a lot of machines going at the same time and would have been thrilled to grow two extra hands. It took me a few tries to get the mix the way I wanted it. As you'll soon discover as you work on your own songs, you often have to learn to "play" a mix as if it were a musical instrument. Practice makes perfect.

The song's bridge, which starts off with the lyric "My friends think it's crazy what she's doing to me" (not the echoey version in the intro), is a good example of vocal stacking. I've forgotten exactly how many vocal tracks I ended up stacking, but I do remember doing a lot of doubling, tripling, and premixing. I was trying to get that Roy Thomas Baker sound, as you might hear in a song like Queen's "Bohemian Rhapsody."

The highest harmony especially needed tripling, because that part was really too high for me to reach. As a result, I often strained to hit the notes. No one take was useable, but by singing that high harmony three times and mixing the takes together, I managed to smooth out the part enough to make it sound reasonably good. I freely admit I'm not the greatest singer in the world, but I was (and still am) pretty thrilled with the way those stacked vocals came out. By the way, the vocals on the choruses were doubled and panned slightly left and right.

Case Study #2

"Take Another Look"
by Mung Brothers
© 1999 by Dan Palladino and Rich Gantner
Case study by Dan Palladino

"Take Another Look" was recorded in two separate studios using Alesis ADATs (digital tape recorders) synced up to a Mac G3 running MOTU Digital Performer (multitrack recording software).

The drum and percussion tracks were triggered, via MIDI, by the sequencer in Digital Performer. The bass guitar track was recorded direct (not using a mic, but rather plugging directly into the mixer), with compression being applied during tracking.

The acoustic guitar at the beginning of the tune was recorded in a long hallway with a high ceiling, using a large condenser mic close to the neck at the twelfth fret. Another large condenser mic was positioned about eight feet in front of the guitar, at a height of six feet, to capture the ambiance of the hallway. The two signals were panned opposite each other, with the close mic a little more prominent on the right side.

A clean electric guitar with chorus was panned to the left to balance out the acoustic. On the choruses, two additional overdriven guitars were panned opposite each other. These tracks were recorded using two completely different guitar/amp combinations to give them some tonal variation.

All vocals were recorded using an Audio Technica 4033 large condenser mic, through an ART Dual MP pre-amp, to an ART PRO-VLA compressor. The signal was recorded directly to tape, bypassing the mixer. The first verse was single-tracked. The remaining vocals were double-tracked, but with the doubles being much lower in volume. This was done to minimize the chorus effect of the doubling. The swirling effect during the breakdown section was achieved using patch #1 on the Lexicon MPX-1 multieffects unit. The patch contains a wahlike filter, auto-panning, and some reverb. All the harmony vocals were bounced down to two tracks (premixed), along with the Lexicon effect.

Case Study #3

"Misdirection"
by Clay Walnum
© 1998 by Clayton Walnum
Case study by Clayton Walnum

I'm a huge Beatles fan, and this song is kind of a nod to that phenomenal group. The main part of the song is John Lennon–ish. The long outro, on the other hand, is inspired by the end of one of my favorite Beatles songs, "I Want You (She's So Heavy)," although my version's ending is nowhere near as dark as the way The Beatles ended their song. In any case, the whole idea with the extended outro is to build up to an intense climax. But I'm getting ahead of myself.

Let's start with the song itself. The lead vocal is tripled, with a voice in the center, one to the left, and one to the right. In the choruses, three vocal parts still spread across the stereo spectrum, but the ones on the left and right become harmonies, yielding a three-part harmony section. The same is true of the bridge (the part that starts with the lyric "Why can't I say the way I feel," right before the guitar solo.)

As for the guitars, I play the electric on the right through a tremolo effect. We didn't cover tremolo when we talked about effects earlier in the book. For those who don't know, tremolo is related to vibrato, except that tremolo quickly varies the volume of an instrument, whereas vibrato varies the pitch of an instrument. Besides the electric guitar, a subtle acoustic guitar part hides in the center of the mix, tucked in behind the vocal.

This is another older song, like "She's Tall Enough (For Me)," so the drums are a drum machine. I recorded this song before I got into drum loops, which can make a huge difference in how your songs sound. (Listen to "Feeling Moody," also in the Case Studies folder, to see what I mean.) In this case, though, I think the drum machine works okay, because I didn't try to program anything too fancy, mostly just a straight beat.

The long ending was pretty much a cut-and-paste job. First, I recorded the basic tracks for 12 bars of the ending. Then, I made a copy of the tracks and added the first new instrument (the maracas in the center of the mix) to the copy. Now I had two, 12-bar sections. I made a copy of this new, second section and added yet another instrument, this time the orchestral chords. This copying and instrument-adding process continued until I had the full set of 12-bar sections, which I then spliced together in a digital audio editor. *Voilà!*

Case Study #4

"Walk On"
by Mung Brothers
© 1999 by Dan Palladino and Rich Gantner
Case study by Dan Palladino

"Walk On" was recorded in two separate studios, using Alesis ADATs (digital multitrack tape recorders) synced up to a Mac G3 running MOTU Digital Performer (multitrack recording software similar to Pro Tools Free).

The drum tracks were triggered, via MIDI, by an Alesis MMT-8 sequencer. The drums were then recorded onto ADAT tape and synced to the computer, running MOTU Digital Performer. The bass guitar track was recorded direct, with compression being applied during tracking. During mixdown, the bass track was re-amped (using a Music Man tube amplifier) and recorded back into the computer with a Shure SM57 dynamic mic. The two signals were then combined during mixdown.

The acoustic guitar at the beginning of the tune was recorded using a large condenser mic close to the neck at the twelfth fret. A direct line (no mic, but rather plugged directly into the mixer) was also recorded, coming from the guitar's built-in pickup system. The two signals were combined to create the final acoustic sound. The electric guitar with the tremolo effect during the verses was a preset on the POD amplifier simulator. On the choruses, two additional overdriven guitars were panned opposite each other. These tracks were recorded using two completely different guitar/POD combinations.

The lead vocal was recorded using an Audio Technica 4033 large condenser mic, through an ART Dual MP pre-amp, to an ART PRO-VLA compressor. The signal was recorded directly to tape, bypassing the mixer. Background vocals, which were all double-tracked, were recorded using a Neumann TLM-103 mic. The panning effect on the lead vocal that leads into the final choruses was achieved using an auto-pan program in a Lexicon PCM-81 multieffects unit.

Case Study #5

"Feeling Moody"
by Clay Walnum
© 1998 by Clayton Walnum
Case study by Clayton Walnum

Currently, I use drum loops for all my drum tracks. Because they're real drums recorded in a professional studio, drum loops make a huge difference in your song's overall sound when compared with the same tracks recorded from a drum machine. This song, which boasts crankin' drums, is a great example of what I mean.

Depending on the library you choose, drum loops come in various lengths, from simple four-beat patterns to parts that are several minutes long. To assemble the drum tracks for "Feeling Moody," I used a digital audio editor on my computer to cut and paste various loops to create verse, chorus, and bridge parts, then assembled those parts into my song arrangement using the same audio editor. (I believe the software I used was Sonic Foundry's Sound Forge.) When the drum tracks were assembled, I transferred them to my Roland VS-1680, all-in-one workstation. Then it was "just" a matter of adding the remaining tracks over the drums.

The lead vocal is a single voice panned to the center, with a harmony vocal, also panned to the center, on every other line. The lead vocal in the chorus, on the other hand, is doubled with each voice panned left and right. In addition, there's a short, three-part harmony part, with all voices panned center, that "answers" lines in the chorus. If I remember correctly, the vocals on this one were recorded using a trusty Shure SM57 mic.

The bass guitar, as with almost everything I record, is panned to the center and was recorded using a bass Sans Amp (an amp simulator) plugged directly into the recorder. (I love the sound of the bass on this song.) The other guitar parts were also recorded directly into the recorder, first going through a Line 6 POD amp simulator, which I currently use for all my recorded guitar parts. I don't even own a guitar amp anymore. Unless you're playing in a band, amp simulators like the POD give you everything you need, and you don't have to wake up the whole town when you're recording late at night.

The undistorted electric guitar parts in the verses were played twice, with each guitar panned left and right. In the choruses, the same is true of the distorted guitar chords. The weird guitar solo after the second chorus (the guitar is supposed to sound angry and moody) was electronically doubled using delay, with each image panned left and right. A lot of doubling is going on in this song, done either electronically or by playing each part twice. In fact, the lead-guitar fills right after the first chorus were about the only guitar parts not doubled, with the guitar lines alternating left and right in the mix.

Mixing to Disk with Automation

Typically, you record your final mix by sending the output of your multitrack recorder to some sort of stereo machine such as a digital audio tape (DAT) recorder, a cassette recorder (not recommended), or even another computer. Pro Tools, however, lets you mix to the same disk on which you recorded your sessions (or any other disk, for that matter) with the Bounce to Disk command.

First, set up your mix and get it ready to go. Everything has to be just right, because once you start the bounce-to-disk function, Pro Tools will not let you change any settings until the bounce is complete. When you have your mix ready, perform the following steps. Note that these steps assume you want your final mix in the right format to burn to CD:

1. Select the Bounce to Disk command from the File menu, as shown in Figure F.1. When you do, the Bounce dialog box appears.

2. Change the Format setting to Stereo Interleaved, as shown in Figure F.2.

3. Change the resolution to 16-bit (Figure F.3).

4. Click the Bounce button. Pro Tools asks for the mix's file name (Figure F.4). You can name the file anything you want.

5. After typing the file name, click the Save button. Pro Tools plays the session and records the result to the file you chose, as shown in Figure F.5.

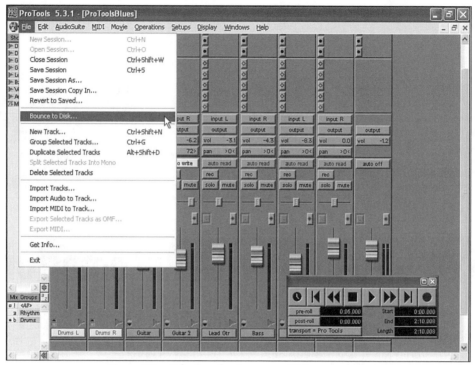

Figure F.1   Selecting the Bounce to Disk command.

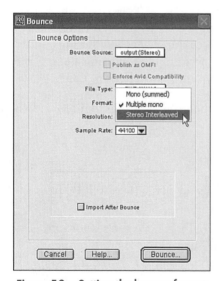

Figure F.2   Setting the bounce format.

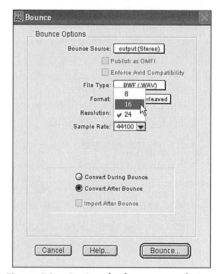

Figure F.3   Setting the bounce resolution.

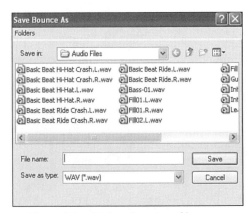

Figure F.4   Giving the mix a file name.

Figure F.5   Pro Tools performing the bounce.

Easy enough, right? You might, however, come across one major stumbling block. Remember that Pro Tools will not allow you to change mix settings during the bounce. What if your mix requires you to do something like change the volume of a channel or manipulate the panning as the mix is going on? Automation to the rescue!

You can set up Pro Tools so it remembers just about everything you do as you prepare a mix. For example, suppose you need to adjust the volume of tracks 3 and 4 as the mix is recording. First, set the tracks to write automation data by clicking the tracks' automation buttons and setting them to Auto Write, as shown in Figure F.6. Now, if you make changes to these tracks during the mix, Pro Tools automatically remembers what to do.

When you're done setting up the mix, click the automation button again and set it to Auto Read. When you start your bounce to disk, Pro Tools reenacts your changes. You can even see the faders moving up and down on the screen.

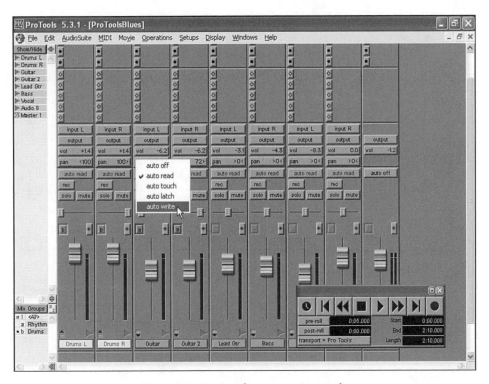

Figure F.6   Setting the automation mode.

About This Book's Disc

The disc that accompanies this book contains everything you need to get started with your own recording projects—except for Pro Tools Free, which you can download from the Digidesign website at www.digidesign.com. Here's a quick overview of the CD's contents:

> Folders Chapter06 through Chapter15 contain the files for the associated chapters' projects.
>
> The Case Studies folder contains the songs that go with Appendix E.
>
> Finally, the Waves folder contains the trial versions of the Waves plug-ins for Pro Tools.

You can transfer all the files from the disc using the included setup program. To perform this installation, follow these steps:

1. Open your Start menu.
2. Select the Run command.
3. In the Run box, type your CD drive's drive letter, followed by a colon and **Setup.** For example, if your CD-ROM drive is drive D, you'd type **D:Setup.**
4. Press Enter, and the setup program will run.
5. Follow the setup program's instructions to install the CD-ROM's contents onto your hard drive.

Index

WARRANTY LIMITS

READ THE ENCLOSED AGREEMENT AND THIS LABEL BEFORE OPENING SOFTWARE MEDIA PACKAGE.

BY OPENING THIS SEALED CD-ROM PACKAGE, YOU ACCEPT AND AGREE TO THE TERMS AND CONDITIONS PRINTED BELOW. IF YOU DO NOT AGREE, **DO NOT OPEN THE PACKAGE.** SIMPLY RETURN THE SEALED PACKAGE.

This content CD-ROM is distributed on an "AS IS" basis, without warranty. Neither the author, the publisher, and/or Penguin Group (USA) Inc./Alpha Books make any representation or warranty, either express or implied, with respect to the content CD-ROM, its quality, accuracy, or fitness for a specific purpose. Therefore, neither the author, the publisher, and/or Penguin Group (USA) Inc./Alpha Books shall have any liability to you or any other person or entity with respect to any liability, loss, or damage caused directly or indirectly by the content contained on the content CD-ROM or by the CD-ROM itself. If the content CD-ROM is defective, you may return it for replacement.